Britain's World of Steam

Paul Catchpole

A Locomotives International Publication

Above: 2-6-2T no. 31 from the Jokioisten Railway in Finland arriving on a low-loader. Photo courtesy of the Welshpool & Llanfair Light Railway.

Front Cover: (clockwise from top left) 'Kriegslok' 2-10-0 no. Ty2-7173 at Wansford on the Nene Valley Railway, 0-8-0T 'Sir Drefaldwyn' on the Welshpool & Llanfair Narrow Gauge Railway, Hunslet 0-4-2T 'Chaka's Kraal No. 6' at Toddington on the North Gloucestershire Narrow Gauge Railway, Beyer Peacock 2-6-2+2-6-2 Garratt no. 138 on the Welsh Highland Railway.

Rear Cover: (left) A Kerr Stuart 'Joffre' class 0-6-0T overlooking Blaenau Ffestiniog from Gloddfa Ganol. (Right) Orenstein & Koppel 0-6-0T no. 740 at Amberley Chalk Pits after arrival from India.

Title Page: The Exmoor Steam Railway is now home to this two foot gauge Garratt but S.A.R. no. 115 is seen here working a goods train when still in South Africa. Photo: Brian Rumary.

© 2002 *Locomotives International* and Paul Catchpole.
All rights reserved. No part of this book may be reproduced or transmitted in any form or by any means without prior written permission from the publisher.

ISBN 1-900340-14-3
First Edition. Published by Paul Catchpole Ltd., The Haven, Trevilley Lane, St. Teath, Cornwall, PL30 3JS, Great Britain.
www.locomotivesinternational.co.uk
Printed and bound by Tiskárna Dr. Eduard Grégr a syn, Prague, Czech Republic.
British Library Cataloguing in Publication Data. A catalogue record for this book is available from the British Library.

Britain's World of Steam
Paul Catchpole

Contents

Introduction	4
British Railways Locomotives, Back Home	10
Locomotives Sent Abroad During the First World War	15
American Locomotives of the Great War Period	17
The German Narrow Gauge 'Feldbahn' (Field Railway)	20
British War Department Locomotives Repatriated	22
United States Army Transport Corps 'Over Here'	25
Exports to the Empire, Repatriated	28
Out of Africa - Garratts Large and Small	32
Out of Africa - 3'6" 'Cape' Gauge and Narrow Gauge	35
Locomotives Built Abroad for Service in Britain	45
Main Line Steam From Scandinavia	48
Main Line Steam From France and Germany	55
Polish Industrials in Britain	57
East European Narrow Gauge Locomotives	60
West European Narrow Gauge Locomotives	62
Orenstein & Koppel Narrow Gauge Locomotives	65
Narrow Gauge Steam From Spanish Lines	68
The Guinness Brewery Locomotives	71
15" Gauge Locomotives	72
Steam Tram Locomotives	73
Narrow Gauge Sugar Plantation Steam	74
Index by Builder	90

Thanks and acknowledgements:

Many people have each contributed a little information which all put together has amounted to this book. Some have also assisted with photographs, so where a picture has been provided by someone other than the author the photographer's name is credited in the caption. For additional information and for their support for this publication and over a long period for 'Locomotives International' in general, special appreciation is due to Harry Wright, Trevor Rowe, Paul Cotterell and Keith Taylorson.

Further to this, for responding to enquiries I wish to thank the Romney, Hythe & Dymchurch Railway, Strumpshaw Hall, the Welshpool & Llanfair Light Railway, South Tynedale Railway, Welsh Highland Railway (Porthmadog), Ffestiniog Railway, and the Brecon Mountain Railway. My thanks also to the staff and volunteers at every single railway centre (and builders merchant) featured in this book, as my enquiries on site visits have only ever been rewarded by a friendly and helpful response.

The information in this book has been pieced together over more than 20 years, bit by tiny bit, partly by word of mouth but also from more magazine articles and odd snippets in books than I can even remember, let alone list here, but particularly worthy of mention have been Roger Crombleholme and Terry Kirtland's enthusiasts' handbooks published by 'Steam Past' in the 1980s and the Industrial Railway Society's meticulously created and maintained Industrial Locomotives handbooks, published every four years.

Finally, a big thanks to my wife Sue for supporting me in producing this book and to my sons Edward & Matthew who thoroughly enjoyed their ride in the lookout of the Brecon Mountain Railway's caboose!

Introduction

The Influx of Locomotives

Steam locos have been coming here from abroad for many years now for one reason or another, though with such a large quantity of capable railway builders in the country only a very few were ever built specifically for export to Britain. By far the majority have arrived since the 1960s, shipped into our ports on the surge of steam railway enthusiasm. This is particularly so in the case of narrow gauge examples whose purchase and recovery is more feasibly within the economic range of an individual or a small group. For this reason there are many more narrow gauge locomotives in this book than standard or broad gauge.

As far as standard gauge locos are concerned it is worth considering why they are being imported at all, when there are so many rescued from Barry Island or industrial railways still rusting in preservation society sidings. One answer must be the cost of putting a corroded engine back in steam, which can run into tens of thousands of pounds even if nothing major is found wrong during restoration. On top of this are the months, or more likely years, of work which have to go into a project of this scale.

As an alternative, a comparable main line locomotive can often be purchased out of store or even out of service from a foreign railway at a reasonable price, complete with any spare parts for future use. The cost then of shipping it will be cheaper, and the return to steam quicker than if a restoration job is undertaken, with the result that the fare-paying public will be riding behind, paying for the upkeep that much sooner. Of course some people like to do it the hard way and buy a wreck of a loco from somewhere half way round the globe! This can still be worthwhile though in the case of some unique and historically important specimens which would otherwise be lost for good.

A significant factor governing the import of steam from overseas must be the number of enthusiasts who over the years have been packing their bags and going off to strange places in search of locos in action. Sometimes the object has been to find British-built locos exported during Empire or Commonwealth periods, sometimes to see more exotic machines that take the eye some getting used to, with all the pumps, pipes and bits festooned about the boiler. Either way an interest in locos working overseas has been generated, and enthusiasts are wanting to see their favourite types nearer home. The withdrawal from stock of these locos has now made this a possibility, and furthermore there won't be any uncomprehending and incomprehensible men in uniforms to make life difficult for the photographer. How many gricers have had film confiscated or a visit refused, and returned home to find a museum railway has just taken delivery of a similar type of engine ?!

If a steam loco is wanted for a narrow gauge line there may be no choice other than to import one. With a finite number of surviving locos and an expanding number of narrow gauge railways, they have got to be built new or brought in. The Talyllyn Railway has managed to do both at the same time by obtaining an ex-Bord na Mona 3 foot gauge 0-4-0WT from Eire and using some of the main components to construct a new 2'3" gauge loco.

This WD 2-10-0, no. 3672, was repatriated from Greece, the only country which still had some unpreserved examples of these British-built locomotives.

Gauge and Size

In European countries such as France and Germany, there have been extensive narrow gauge systems and hence, a larger pool of motive power to draw upon for preservation. With the closure of lines in Poland we could perhaps see more tender locos arriving in the future - some of our Great Little Railways are tending to the 'great' as far as length is concerned and the Px48 class 0-8-0 would be suitable motive power for some lines.

Meanwhile India has proved to be a source of redundant tank locos as may Indonesia and Romania too, but the richest pickings have been from South Africa and Mozambique. A large quantity of former sugar plantation locomotives and larger engines from the South African Railways 2' gauge lines can now be seen in Britain, many of them having been built at British locomotive works.

It is possible for narrow gauge locomotives from various countries intended for slightly differing track widths to run in this country with little problem. Where the gauges concerned are 1'11½", 2 foot, or 600 mm, the differences are fairly minimal as the distance across the wheel flange is always slightly less than the rail gauge anyway, indeed some railways are laid to all three widths depending on where on the line you take the measurement! Locomotives constructed to these gauges are designed to run on roughly laid tracks of country or quarry lines and are virtually interchangeable between the different widths. On sharp curves a certain liberalism is necessary to enable the engines to get round, as the squealing and creaking will often testify. The principle of interchange between metric and imperial gauges also applies to the 2'6" gauge of the Welshpool & Llanfair Light Railway, which can take rolling stock built to 760 mm gauge.

Where the real problems occur is with the Berne Gauge, used throughout Europe as the standard loading gauge. Although the rail gauge is the same as in Britain, the allowances for height and width are considerably greater, so the clearances on most preserved lines are insufficient to take the continental rolling stock. Even ex-Great Western routes tend to be too tight, so to establish a railway for full-size European locos to work on it is necessary to find a route with high bridge and tunnel clearances, and either clear the line of any trackside encumbrances or relay it with a sufficient width allowance. These measures have been taken on the Nene Valley Railway and the Bo'ness & Kinneil Railway, where continental coaching stock is also run, however, not all European locos were built to maximum dimensions, so some of them, such as the Polish industrial 0-6-0 and 0-8-0 tank locos can be run on other lines.

Even the 3'6" gauge track in Africa has rolling stock too large for the standard British loading gauge! A proposal by the Plym Valley Railway (an ex-GWR line) to build a dual standard and 3'6" gauge track along its route to accommodate a massive Garratt from South Africa unfortunately fell through and the few locomotives of this gauge in the UK have little prospect of

A 600 mm gauge 0-8-0T at Toddington on the North Gloucestershire Narrow Gauge line. This size of loco is suitable for lines of modest length but also has the pulling power and water capacity to cope with heavier demands.

running again in the forseeable future.

The metre gauge takes more moderately proportioned rolling stock, but nevertheless it has been necessary to build a line specially to this size, although the atmosphere is more that of an oversized narrow gauge line. This gauge has been established at a small steam centre in Irchester Country Park, Northamptonshire to accommodate some former ironstone railway locomotives of metre gauge but could potentially provide a focal point for the collection of more metre gauge equipment from abroad, perhaps Mallets from Portugal or Pacifics from India?

This Swedish B Class 4-6-0 was stored in the country's strategic reserve and so was in a relatively good condition when purchased. It was back in steam after just a few months but due to its size can only run on lines able to take rolling stock built to the Continental loading gauge.

One of the few 3'6" gauge locos in Britain, Rhodesia Railways No. 993, and behind it possibly the only coach built to that gauge in the country. During restoration they were accommodated on a specially constructed length of track in the grounds of Whipsnade Park.

Getting To See Particular Locomotives

This can be a problem, especially if an enthusiast wants to find the loco in steam, or even just in one piece. Many of the larger imported locos are complete as major renovations have tended to be unnecessary unless they have been at work in preservation for some years. It is a different matter though in the case of smaller locomotives from industrial or agricultural railways. Often these arrive in a very poor state, and may have been operated during their final days of commercial service in a very run-down mechanical condition. It can take many years of work and expense to repair such a loco, and the undertaking is truly a labour of love on the part of the enthusiast.

Once the initial major restoration by new owners has been completed the upkeep becomes easier and periods out of action shorter. Of course all locos have to have lesser items of servicing done from time to time, and may be found with boiler tubes out or rods down etc. for a while, so it is worth phoning the steam centre concerned before starting any long journeys, to ensure the relevant engine(s) are on view. The transportability of small narrow gauge locos also makes it advisable to check whether a particular engine is still on site where it was last seen. The plus side to this is that privately preserved locomotives not always on public view may visit narrow gauge railways for gala weekends or other special events.

Left: Fowler 0-4-2T 'Saccharine' was found largely intact and in good repair at the Alford Valley Railway in the Highlands of Scotland. It was the first time I had seen one of these Fowlers, produced in some numbers for agricultural and industrial lines, but on the day of my visit the loco wasn't in the easiest of locations for photography!

'Barbouilleur' was in the latter stages of restoration when seen in the Amberley Chalk Pits Museum workshop some years ago. This loco is only operated for the public a few times a year at her base on the Bredgar & Wormshill line in Kent but from time to time has been transported to other lines for special events.

Fortunately many private owners will have a few days in the year when they open up for public steamings and a letter with a stamped, addressed envelope will usually elicit a response, with a warm welcome on the open days. Where locos are only seen by prior arrangement it is essential out of common courtesy that the owner is contacted, and that private property is respected as such - to suffer uninvited visitors turning up every weekend is not everybody's cup of tea!

There are a very few locomotives that are just not on view to the public at all, but that's the owner's wish and prerogative. These locomotives are stored behind closed doors and intrusions into privacy will only cause offence. I am sure that every loco at some stage in its life comes into public view.

So, not every repatriated steam locomotive is illustrated in this book, and some of them have never steamed since first I started seeking them out over 25 years ago! Most though are shown, having been found substantially complete at one time or another, and I hope the reader will enjoy this look at the astounding variety of steam locos to be found in Britain today.

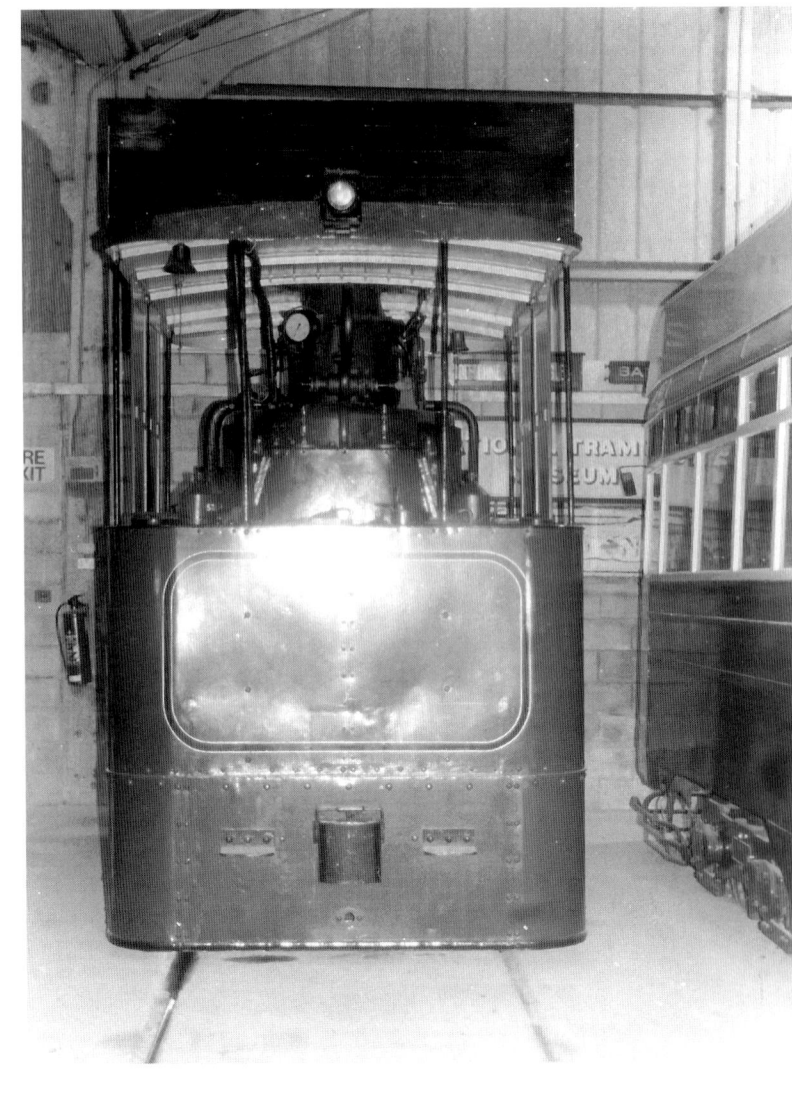

Right: Not in use on the day but at least this steam tram was in one piece and on show in the shed when a visit was made to the National Tramway Museum at Crich in Derbyshire. This is the only British-built steam tram in the country and it is maintained in operating condition by the museum.

This 2-8-2 on the Welsh Highland Railway has been dismantled for restoration at Porthmadog since this photo was taken. As with most railway workshops, Gelert's Farm is not open to the public to wander round as it is subject to Health & Safety regulations, but no doubt the loco will be on view and better still, active, in due course.

Out of the 485 'Austerity' 0-6-0 saddle tanks built, 377 were supplied to the War Department. Some of these were sent over to the Continent after D-Day and of these a few have survived into the preservation era. One such is the Bodmin & Wenford Railway's 'Swiftsure', built by Hunslet in 1943 (works no. 2857). As WD no. 75008 this loco worked in Belgium based at Antwerpen Dam shed in order to shunt on Antwerp docks before returning to Britain in 1946 and going into service with the National Coal Board.

The import of a 2 foot gauge USA-built Baldwin Pacific from South Africa has enabled the Brecon Mountain Railway to capture the atmosphere of an American narrow gauge short line, aided by the addition of a replica Sandy River railroad caboose built in the BMR's own workshops.

Also from the African continent, but decidedly British in style, the Welshpool & Llanfair's selection of repatriated and overseas locos includes No. 14, a Hunslet 2-6-2T that originally worked as no. 85 for the Sierra Leone Government Railways.

British Railways Locomotives, Back Home

Quite a number of familiar locomotives have worked abroad at some time in their lives. A few of them went overseas with the army during the First and Second World Wars and are documented in the appropriate chapter. Others have been out of Britain during the preservation era for prolonged periods due to extended tours or having been purchased abroad then sold back to British owners. For example, Great Western Railway 4-6-0 4079 'Pendennis Castle' spent over twenty years in Australia.

Following the end of steam on British Railways, the 'Flying Scotsman' toured America and Australia and other former B.R. locomotives were privately purchased for display in the States, two of which have since returned. Shorter visits to foreign rails have been made for special events, such as when the Great Western 'City of Truro' visited Holland for the Dutch 150th anniversary of railways in 1989 and when locomotives owned by the National Railway Museum were exhibited in Japan. More recently Terrier class 0-6-0T 'Fenchurch' has been running on the Stoomtram Hoorn Medemblik line in Holland and Leighton Buzzard Narrow Gauge locos 'Pixie' and 'Peter Pan' have been in Belgium visiting the Maldegem Steam Centre.

During the 1920s and 1930s several British locomotives visited America for exhibitions and amid great publicity hauled trains throughout the USA. To meet railroad regulations and run with US rolling stock they were fitted with a bell and headlight and in the case of the 'Royal Scot' and 'King Class' 4-6-0s a cow-catcher or 'pilot' in American parlance was also carried.

4-6-0 GWR No. 6000 'King George V'

The Great Western Railway's 'King George V', known colloquially as 'KGV' was the first of the main line locomotives to cross the Atlantic to the USA, invited to the Baltimore & Ohio Railroad's centenary in August 1927. Outshopped from construction at Swindon works in June, only a few weeks before departure, 6000 was the Great Western's flagship locomotive of it's express passenger fleet, however, by American standards it was a small locomotive and is said to have been mistaken by some of the US railwaymen for a shunting engine! Fortunately the opportunity to perform on the main line sorted out the misconception in no uncertain terms when a 544-ton train was worked between Baltimore and Philadelphia at up to 74 mph (119 km/h).

Great Western 4-6-0 'King George V' seen at Swindon shed when still in regular service in the early 1960s. Note the bell on the buffer beam. Photo: Geoffrey Jones.

During the centenary celebrations 6000 carried a headlight, bell and cow-catcher and led the locomotive parades. The headlight and cow-catcher were removed afterwards but the GWR allowed 'KGV' to retain the bell, proudly carried on the buffer beam to this day.

Such was the respect held by this locomotive that it was given a special dispensation to run on the main line on a tour that was to start the return of steam traction to the main line. Hauling the Bulmers Cider Co. rake of Pullman coaches from Tyseley to Didcot in October 1971 on this railtour, 6000 was seen by the author passing Wadleys Bridge, Solihull, an event which triggered a life-long interest in steam and led to many memorable railway adventures.

6000 is now kept at the 'Steam' museum at Swindon.

4-6-0 LMSR No. 6100 'Royal Scot'

The second locomotive to do an American tour was the London Midland and Scottish Railway's pride of the line, 6100 'Royal Scot', sent over for the Chicago Exhibition of 1933. The three-cylinder 'Royal Scot' class express locos were built from 1927 onwards to haul a prestige passenger train of that name between London and Scotland and the LMSR decided to send out not just the locomotive but the whole train.

In point of fact the actual locomotive that visited America was not the original 6100 but was sister engine 6152 'King's Dragoon Guardsman' built at Derby in 1929. The identities were swapped over prior to the exhibition and were never swapped back, so the loco preserved at Bressingham Gardens, Diss, is the original 6152 which made the journey to Chicago as 6100.

It has remained as 6100 'Royal Scot', though differing considerably in appearance since then as the loco was substantially rebuilt at Crewe with a taper boiler in June 1950. *(Not illustrated).*

4-6-2 LMSR No. 46229 'Duchess of Hamilton'

The Coronation or Duchess class pacifics of the London Midland and Scottish Railway were designed for running the 'Coronation Scot' non-stop express train between London and Glasgow, inaugurated in 1937. The 'Duchess of Hamilton' was the last of the initial batch of ten streamlined locomotives built in 1937-38, numbered 6229.

In 1939 the LMSR decided to send a complete 'Coronation Scot' train, coaches and all, for a 3,000 mile tour of the USA culminating in display at the New York World's Fair. 6229 was selected as the locomotive and once again identities were swapped with the class leader, in this case 6220 'Coronation'. On this occassion though identities were changed back afterwards, however, the stay in America turned out to be longer than intended. The Duchess did not return to Britain immediately after the end of the World's Fair as the Second World War had broken out in the meantime and it was considered too risky to ship the loco back across the Atlantic. Instead she was stored at Baltimore shed for about two years, returning in February 1942. By then the 'Coronation Scot' service had been suspended and the coaches never ran on their intended train.

The streamlined casing was removed after the war and the number was prefixed to become 46229 upon Nationalisation on 1st January 1948. Early in 1964 the Duchess was withdrawn and purchased by Butlins for display at the Minehead holiday camp, remaining there until loaned to the National Railway Museum in 1975.

With support from the 'Friends of the NRM' the loco was restored to working order in 1980 and the NRM officially acquired 46229 seven years later. It has recently undergone a major overhaul with consideration given to re-applying the streamlining, however, the conventional apperance remains, so far. *(Not illustrated)*.

0-4-4T L&SWR Class M7 No. 30053

M7 0-4-4T no. 30053 stands at the buffers in Swanage station awaiting the chance to steam on Southern metals again after a 21-year stay in America.

Dougal Drummond designed the M7 class for branch line and suburban work on the London and South Western Railway which had 105 examples built in total. 30053 was constructed in 1905 at Nine Elms and was originally numbered 53, the additional 30000 being added after nationalisation of Britain's railways. Over the years in service this loco worked from allocations throughout south-east England, latterly on push-pull trains. The last allocation was to Bournemouth in January 1964. 30053 worked on the Swanage branch, where it is now preserved, during the period up to the end of May that year and last worked on 5th July to participate in a final railtour. Total recorded mileage was 1,786,577.

Luckily 30053 was purchased for the Steamtown Museum at Bellows Falls, Vermont, USA by a Mr. Nelson F. Blount and was refurbished at Eastleigh in 1966. During this overhaul the auto-train gear was removed.

Two Southern Railway locomotives, the M7 and 'Schools' class 4-4-0 'Repton', were shipped from Liverpool to Montreal on the Canadian Pacific ship 'Roonagh Head', departing on 18th April 1967 along with a GWR passenger brake coach. They went on static display at Steamtown, mostly exhibited in the open but received periodic repaints to sustain a reasonable external condition - though not always quite in authentic colours!

Two independent initiatives led ultimately to repatriation of the two Southern Railway locomotives, a letter to the press from a Mr. Colin Hebbes wanting to see if there was support for such a prospect and an approach to Steamtown by the Southern Steam Trust. In 1982 Mr. Hebbes and the SST held a joint public meeting and formed 'Southern Repatriation' and began some protracted negotiations, finally resolved with the despatch of 30053 in February 1987.

The M7 was shipped from New York on the Nedlloyd 'Rosario', arriving at Felixstowe on 6th April 1987. During an overnight stop on the road journey back to Swanage the red coupling rods (!) were painted black and after other cosmetic corrections made over the following few days the loco was put on display. Full restoration to running order was subsequently organised by the Drummond Locomotive Society and undertaken at the Swanage Railway where 30053 is in regular use.

30053 stands outside the shed at Swanage receiving routine maintenance to the rear bogie in May 2002.

4-4-0 SR Schools Class No. 30926 'Repton'

The 3-cylinder 'Schools' class was designed by R.E.L. Maunsell to haul light expresses on the line to Hastings which had a particularly tight loading gauge due to restricted tunnel bores. They were in some respects shortened versions of the 'Lord Nelson' class and were the last main line 4-4-0 type built in Britain, 40 examples appearing between 1930-35. Withdrawal took place 1961-62 so 30926 had already been out of use a few years before being bought for preservation.

'Repton' was restored in Southern livery as no. 926 and in 1967 travelled with 30053 to Steamtown Vermont, but unlike the tank loco, actually saw some active service during its stay, though in Canada, not the USA. While in Steamtown's ownership the loco was lent to the Cape Breton Railway in Nova Scotia and received a cowcatcher, headlight, bell, air brake equipment and a buckeye coupler in order to work trains over part of the former Sydney and Louisberg Railway.

It was some time after 30053's return to the UK before sufficient funds were available to facilitate the repatriation of 'Repton'. Also, instead of returning to familiar metals the 4-4-0 went to the North Yorkshire Moors Railway. After restoration to running order the loco gained a reputation for slipping on the steep inclines, and on the occasion of a visit by the author to this line had to be rescued. It was, after all, intended for quite a different type of service, however, it has remained on the NYMR and has seen plenty of use there.

4-6-2 L&NER Class A3
No. 4472 'Flying Scotsman'

Sir Nigel Gresley's A1 Pacifics were designed just before the 1923 grouping of British railway companies and the 'Flying Scotsman' was the first locomotive to by completed for the newly formed London and North Eastern Railway. Originally the type was classified as A1 but alterations to the valve gear and boiler resulted in re-classification as A3 class. From 1928 some of the A3s received corridor tenders to allow for crew changes when working non-stop trains to Scotland.

Upon nationalisation 4472 was renumbered to 60103. After withdrawal in the 1960s 'Flying Scotsman' was purchased by Alan Pegler and restored to LNER identity and apple green livery. As steam operations disappeared from British Railways watering points were removed from stations so a second tender was adapted to allow long distance runs to be made without problems from lack of facilities. The two tenders became a famous feature in preservation days, adding further to the kudos of this legendary locomotive.

In late 1969 no. 4472 was shipped over to the USA with a few coaches in order to undertake an extensive tour of the country. The stay in America lasted several years, gradually draining finances and the 'Flying Scotsman' ended up stranded in San Francisco until January 1973 when Sir Bill Mc Alpine stepped in to purchase the loco to prevent it from being permanently exiled. 4472 was loaded on board the 'California Star' and welded to the deck of the ship in order to prevent any possibility of it being

30926 'Repton' storms out of Grosmont on the North Yorkshire Moors Railway.

4472 'Flying Scotsman' near Sandgate on a down main line parallel run with Australian streamlined Pacific no. 3801 on 18th March 1989.

Photo: Harry J. Wright.

Back in Britain after the Australian tour, the 'Flying Scotsman' worked for a season on the Severn Valley Railway and is seen here attracting the crowds at Kidderminster station in 1991.

washed overboard and made the journey back to Britain through the Panama Canal.

After arrival home in February 1973 steam was raised to asses the condition of the engine and an overhaul was undertaken. In September that year 'Flying Scotsman' and 'King George V' double headed a homecoming railtour, both carrying their commemorative bells from America and since then 4472 has been in constant demand for tours and periods of hire by museum railways.

In 1988, after requests from Australia, the 'Flying Scotsman' once more went overseas. The tour was a great success and in the September of that year included the feat of heading a train right the way across the continent from Sydney to Perth. 4472 returned home in December the following year, docking at Tilbury aboard the French container ship 'La Perouse'. As a momento of the Australian tour 4472 was given a 5-tone Nathan chime whistle, fitted in addition to its own 2-tone LNER whistle.

These days the 'Flying Scotsman' is in as much demand as ever, often heading the VSOE Pullman trains on excursions.

4-6-0 GWR No. 4079 'Pendennis Castle'

The four cylinder Castle class was developed by C.B. Collett from the earlier Star class for top link express work on the Great Western Railway, the type first appearing in 1923. 4079 was one of the first series, built at Swindon in 1924.

After withdrawal in the mid 1960s 'Pendennis Castle' was preserved at Carnforth depot in Lancashire, far away from the generous loading gauge of the Great Western Railway. The tighter clearances in the north of England prevented the loco from working trains out of its preservation base so in spite of being in main line running order railtour use was infrequent.

In due course 'Pendennis Castle' was sold to the Hammersley Iron Co. in Australia which owned a long standard gauge railway where the engine could be used to its full potential. The prospect of losing the loco caused dismay amongst British fans mindful of the 'Flying Scotsman' having been stranded in America. A farewell tour was run between Tyseley and Didcot at very short notice on 29th May 1977, witnessed by the author a few days before the loco was shipped from Avonmouth docks.

After some years work in Australia 4079 fell out of use due to depletion of the loco's support group. During 1999 a year of sensitive negotiations took place between the Great Western Society and the Hammersley Iron Co. management, by then owned by RTZ, culminating in an agreement which resulted in 'Pendennis Castle' returning to Britain after the turn of the Millennium. The 4-6-0 is now at Didcot and at the time of writing (May 2002) is undergoing an overhaul.

Left: 4079 'Pendennis Castle' on shed at an unidentified location a few years prior to being withdrawn from regular service.
Photo: Geoffrey Jones.

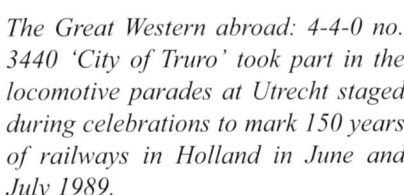

The Great Western abroad: 4-4-0 no. 3440 'City of Truro' took part in the locomotive parades at Utrecht staged during celebrations to mark 150 years of railways in Holland in June and July 1989.

London, Brighton & South Coast Railway 'Terrier' class 0-6-0T no. 672 is seen here shunting on the Bluebell Railway a few years ago but during May 2002 has been active in Belgium and Holland. The Bluebell Railway has now officially twinned with the Dutch Stoomtram Hoorn Medemblik line.

Locomotives Sent Abroad During the First World War

0-6-0 No. 673 'Maude'

Standard gauge. Works no. 4392. Built in 1891 by Neilson at Springburn works for the North British Railway as class 'C'. During the Great War she was shipped to France along with two dozen others of the class. On return they were all given names, and 'Maude' went on to become an LNER class J36, surviving into B.R. days as No.65243. She was withdrawn in 1966 from Bathgate shed and is now maintained by the Scottish Railway Preservation Society for service on the Bo'ness & Kinneil Railway.

0-6-0T W38 'Ajax'

Standard gauge. Andrew Barclay, works no. 1605/1918. This industrial loco was built for the London Sulphide Co. but was requisitioned by the Ministry of Munitions and served overseas during the First World War. Later 'Ajax' worked in Iran for the Anglo-Persian Oil Co. and was at British Steel's Harlaxton plant until 1967. Afterwards the loco was obtained by Henry Frampton-Jones and went into long term storage at the Isle of Wight Steam Railway until finally overhauled in the mid 1990s and renumbered W38. *(Not illustrated)*

Right: 'Maude' is coaled up and ready for her next railtour as she waits in the dim confines of the former headquarters of the SRPS in Falkirk.

2-6-0 GWR 43XX Class No. 5322

Standard gauge. The 43XX class 2-6-0s were designed by G.J. Churchward for mixed traffic work and constructed by the GWR from 1911 till 1932, to a total of 432 examples. No. 5322 was built in 1917 at Swindon and saw use in France during the 1914-18 War, returning afterwards to lead a long life on the Great Western Railway. After withdrawal 5322 ended up in the Barry Island scrapyard but was one of the earlier locomotives to be purchased for preservation. The Great Western Society rescued 5322 in 1969 and have restored her at their Didcot headquarters, where she is now kept.

Below: 5322 outside the shed at Didcot on the occasion of the Great Western Society's 21st anniversary.

0-6-0T 'Joffre' Class Nos. 2405/42/51 and 3010/14

600 mm gauge. Works nos. as above. The first three locos were built in 1915 and the other two in 1916, all by Kerr Stuart for service in France during the Great War. These five 0-6-0Ts are the survivors of a large number of similar locos supplied to the French Artillery, as a result of which the class was named after the then Commander-in-Chief of the French Armies, General Joffre.

All the preserved examples latterly worked for the Carrières De La Valée, Heureseet du Haut Banc in France, no. 2405 going to the West Lancashire Light Railway as no. 9, and the remainder to the North Wales Narrow Gauge Museum at Gloddfa Ganol.

During 1985 one of these, no. 2451 was moved to the Lynton and Barnstaple Railway and named 'Axe'. The L&B is undertaking a rebuild along with the restoration to running order, including provision of a new boiler and conversion to an 0-6-2T to allow a larger cab with a bunker. The large collection at Gloddfa Ganol has since been dispersed with no. 2442 going to the Teifi Valley Railway and at the time of writing no. 3014 is under restoration at Whaley Bridge for the Molesey Tramway.

Above: Kerr Stuart 'Joffre' class 0-6-0T no. 3014 standing sentinel at the entrance to Gloddfa Ganol in the pouring rain. At least this loco had benefitted from a cosmetic restoration in order to attract visitors, and at the time of writing is receiving a full overhaul.

Right: The 2 foot gauge West Lancashire Light Railway also has an example of the class, Kerr Stuart 2405 of 1915, no. 9 in the WLLR roster. This locomotive is also receiving an overhaul and was stripped down in the workshop when seen during the summer of 2001.

Some years ago poor old 3010 was seen suffering the ravages of time and weather sitting amongst the slates of Gloddfa Ganol pending restoration. This loco is now privately preserved in Norfolk.

American Locomotives of the Great War Period

America sent two standard types of narrow gauge tank locomotive over to Europe to serve on the supply lines leading to the front line in France, these were a 2-6-2T and 4-6-0T designs. Examples of both types are preserved in Britain, indeed others exist around the world as they were sold off to industries in Europe and elsewhere after the Armistice.

2-6-2T 'Mountaineer'

600 mm gauge. Built in 1916 by Alco, works no. 57156 and sent to France where WD number 1265, was given, 'Mountaineer' was purchased by the Tramway Pithiviers-Toury in 1935 and re-numbered 3.23. The main use on the line at Pithiviers was for hauling sugar beet freights. Following closure in 1964, enthusiast John Ransom purchased the loco and it arrived on the Ffestiniog Railway in 1967. When a later restoration took place engineer Phil Girdlestone followed the principle established by L.D. Porta of making minor improvements to the various components and machining to accurate tolerances, resulting not only in a more reliable locomotive but a staggering 60% increase in haulage power. Since the re-opening of the northern part of the Welsh Highland Railway route 'Mountaineer' has been working on this line in turn with 'Russel' and the Garratts referred to later.

'Mountaineer' at Boston Lodge Works on the Ffestiniog Railway in Wales.

Several minor variations in external appearance occurred when the 1990s overhaul occurred, as can be seen by comparison between this earlier view at Tan-y-Bwlch and the one above.

4-6-0T Class 101D
'Lion' and 'Tiger'

600 mm gauge. Built by Baldwin, 'Tiger' in 1916 and 'Lion' in 1917. Originally this class of loco was constructed to work on the supply lines in France during the Great War, but later several found use on light railways in Britain. 'Lion' and 'Tiger' went further afield to India, where their history included service at the Upper India Sugar Mills, Khatauli and then Triveni Steelworks. At Khautauli 'Lion' was no. 1 and 'Tiger' was no. 2. In 1985 the two locos were shipped to Britain and upon arrival 'Lion' (Baldwin 44699/1917) went to the Amberley Chalk Pits Museum and 'Tiger' (Baldwin 44656/1916) to the Imperial War Museum at Duxford. An overhaul to working is order of 'Lion' is to be undertaken at the Leighton Buzzard Narrow Gauge Railway.

Triveni Steelworks no. 16 'Lion' at Amberley Chalk Pits Museum shortly after arrival from India.

Baldwin 4-6-0T No. 1 'Lion' seen in India when in service for the sugar mill at Khatauli in March 1979. Photo: Lawrence G. Marshall (courtesy of Keith Taylorson).

The other 4-6-0T from Triveni Steelworks, 'Tiger', as temporarily stored in the grounds of the Imperial War Museum at Duxford pending restoration.

'Tiger' pictured working for the Upper India Sugar Mills, probably in the 1970s.
(Photo courtesy of Keith Taylorson).

By the time this photo was taken in February 1984 'Tiger' was working for Triveni Engineering. It looks as though the loco may have been repainted and the cab is sitting on the loco at a different angle!
Photo: Lawrence G. Marshall (courtesy of Keith Taylorson)

The German Narrow Gauge 'Feldbahn' (Field Railway)

0-4-0WT No. 2

600 mm gauge. Works no. 7529. Built in 1914 by Orenstein & Koppel for use behind the German trenches, and found many years later working in a sand quarry at Nemurs, south of Paris. No. 2 was photographed during restoration at the Cadeby Light Railway, where the owner, John Lucas, had spent much time working on the loco with encouragement from the late Rev. 'Teddy' Boston. It is now on the Golden Valley Railway at Butterly Park, part of the Midland Railway Centre in Derbyshire.

No. 1091 runs round its train in the loop at the North Gloucestershire Narrow Gauge Railway, Toddington, Gloucs. Having seen some years of use, this loco is was set aside for an overhaul at the end of the 2001 operating season.

0-8-0T 'Feldbahn' Class Nos. 6 and 1091

600mm gauge. These two interesting locomotives are examples of a standard type, around 2,500 of which were built to haul supply trains over the field railways to the German side of the trenches in World War 1. In view of the light construction of the railways with tight curves and the need to provide adequate haulage power, an 0-8-0 design was chosen incorporating Klein-Lindner axles which allow side-play of the outer axles combined with some radial movement within the outside frames. (see 'Steam and Rail in Indonesia' for a more detailed description of narrow gauge locomotive articulation).

No. 6 was built in 1918 by

Henschel (works no. 8310) and is now kept at Durley, home of the Hampshire Narrow Gauge Society.

No. 1091 was Henschel works no. 15968 of 1918. Many Feldbahn 0-8-0Ts found their way to 600mm gauge railways in Europe and even beyond, hence 1091 formerly worked in Poland at the Naklo Sugar Factory. It was retrieved in a derelict state, arriving at Toddington in October 1985 but has been restored and operational on the North Goucestershire Narrow Gauge Railway at Toddington, carrying a grey livery. After the 2001 summer season a heavy overhaul will be due which will unfortunately keep it out of traffic for some time.

Several other 'Feldbahn' 0-8-0Ts arrived from a sugar plantation in Mozambique during 1999/2000 and are listed in the final chapter.

0-8-0T No. 10 'Sir Drefaldwyn'

760 mm gauge. Works no. 2855. Built in 1944 by the Societe Franco-Belge de Materiel de Chemins de Fer, this loco was purchased by the Austrian Salzkamergut Lokalbahn and became their no. 19 until closure when it was taken into the stock of Steyrmarkische Landesbahnen as 699.01. It was in this form, running on the Zillertalbahn from Jenbach that the loco was obtained for the Welshpool and Llanfair Light Railway in 1970 and was subsequently given the name 'Sir Drefaldwyn' and a new number.

Right: Single line tokens are exchanged as 'Sir Drefaldwyn' arrives at Sylfaen station on its way to Llanfair Caerinion in September 1999.

'Sir Drefaldwyn' pulls forward out of the headshunt at the Welshpool end of the line to run round to the front of the train.

British War Department Locomotives Repatriated

2-8-0 LMS Class 8F No. 8233, TCDD 'Churchill' Class No. 45160

Standard gauge. 8F no. 8233 carries works no. 24607, built in 1940 by the North British Locomotive Co. for the War Department. This is perhaps the most travelled steam engine in Britain, (and the only one to have suffered a collision with a camel), firstly running on the LMS until 1941, then sent to Iran as no. 307, becoming Iranian State Railways no. 41.109, returning to the W.D. for service in Egypt as no. 70307, back to Longmoor Military Railway as no. 500 in 1952, sold to British Railways in 1957, who numbered it first 90733, then 48773, and finally to the Severn Valley Railway as LMS no. 8233, where it has remained longer than anywhere else!

The 8F from Turkey was built as WD 348 by North British in 1940, (works number 24648), and was one of twenty examples that served in Turkey. They were provided by the Ministry of Supply, and nicknamed the 'Churchill' class by TCDD locomen. Many years ago an interesting account of their delivery via Syria was related to me. As Turkey was theoretically neutral at this sensitive time British troops could not step on Turkish soil, so the twenty locos were made up into to rakes of ten with the leading and trailing locos in steam. A British driver drove the rear locomotive up to the border and jumped off as a Turkish driver jumped onto the leading engine on the other side. For Turkish conditions the 8Fs were small locos and were regarded as 'handy little shunters'!

45160 itself had sailed out from Liverpool in 1941 on board the 'City of Manilla' and worked in Turkey until 1986. It's return journey, after a TCDD overhaul, commenced with an 890 mile railtour across Turkey from Samsun to Mersin, followed by a sea journey to Immingham and arrival in the UK on 11th June 1989. The loco, purchased from the TCDD after protracted negotiations by a quorum of dedicated enthusiasts, initially went to the Swanage Railway and worked briefly there shortly afterwards. It clearly needed a more thorough overhaul than it had recieved before repatriation and, after an initial move to a private site, is at the time of writing on the Gloucester-Warwickshire Railway with work progressing.

A bid is also now in hand to repatriate TCDD 45153.

Although 8233 has worked in Iran and Egypt as well as for the LMS and BR, this 8F has spent more than half it's life preserved on the Severn Valley Railway, always a firm favourite with locomen and public alike.

In the spring of 1978, no. 8233 pulls out of Bridgnorth on the Severn Valley Railway. This 2-8-0 has also been used on the main line for railtours from time to time.

2-10-0 W.D. Nos. 3652 and 3672 'Dame Vera Lynn'

Standard gauge. Works nos. 25438 and 25458, respectively, built in 1943 and 1944 by North British for War Department service overseas. These two examples of the type were among sixteen eventually sent to Greece, where the SEK (Hellenic State Railways) absorbed them into class Lambda beta as 951 and 960.

Before going abroad, up to March 1944, the WD 2-10-0s were sent to Eastfield shed and run in on main line freight trains in Scotland. They were shipped out to the Middle East afterwards and received some more running in on the Palestine Railways before going into store at Suez. It was in January 1946 that they were taken out of store and supplied to the Greek Railways.

In Greece the locos were converted to right hand drive and

Former W.D. 2-10-0 no. 3672 'Dame Vera Lynn' at work on the North Yorkshire Moors Railway.

Below: Hellenic State Railways no. 960 was not trying to win hearts and minds as it backed smokily into Thessaloniki station on 7th September 1972.
Photo: Paul Cotterell.

received raised cab roofs, presumably for ventilation, and a small semi-circular smoke deflector behind the chimney.

Following protracted negotiations the two 2-10-0s were recovered from a yard near Thessaloniki in 1984, 960 going to the Lavender Line at Isfield in Sussex and 951 to the Mid-Hants Railway, along with an S.160 from Greece. 960 has been renumbered 3672 and Dame Vera Lynn herself unveiled the name plate. 951 was restored as 601 'Sturdee' but after transfer to the North Yorkshire Moors Railway and an overhaul, the loco lost its name and was given the number 90775 which follows the BR numbering series for the class. In this guise a remarkabe mileage has been clocked up. On the first occasion I saw this loco in action it was very authentic with a little grime and knocking rods! However, an overhaul has been under way more recently.

2-8-0 W.D. 'Austerity' 8F Class, S.J. No. 1931

Ex-Swedish Railways 'Austerity' 8F no. 1931 inside Oxenhope shed, photographed in cramped conditions when still in S.J. condition.

Standard gauge. Works no. 5200, built in 1945 by Vulcan Foundry to R.A.Riddle's 'Austerity' 8F specification for the War Department, originally numbered 79257. Netherlands Railways (Nederlands Spoorwegen) purchased this locomotive and took it into their stock after the war as no. 4464, but in June 1953 sold it along to Statens Järnväger, the Swedish railway network. The SJ also had another loco of the same type and numbered the pair as 1930 and 1931 in class G11. They were based at Falun but were too long for the local turntables so the tenders were shortened from three to 4 axles. Whilst in Scandinavia the two locos received an all-enclosed cab, small snowploughs and other local fittings, which, unlike the other W.D. locos repatriated, were for a while retained after the return to steam on the Keighley & Worth Valley Railway. They only worked in Sweden for about five years and in 1958 were sidelined into the country's strategic reserve. 1931 stayed in store for nearly 25 years, until purchased by the Keighley and Worth Valley Railway and repatriated in January 1973.

Reconstruction back to British W.D. condition has been under way for some time, for which purpose a 4-axle ex-W.D. tender chassis was obtained from Holland to enable replacement of the 3-axle SJ tender.

0-6-0ST 'Austerity' class, W.D. Nos. 75006, 75008, 75019, 75030, 75031, 75041, 75050, 75082, 75130, 75178

Standard gauge. A large number of Hunslet 'Austerity' saddle tanks are preserved in Britain, some of which went to France, Belgium and Holland. Three that went to Calais were stored for two years and returned in the spring of 1947 probably unused: nos. 75019, 75141, 75178.

Five locos worked on the docks at Antwerp in Belgium from the Autumn of 1944 till Spring 1946, based at Antwerp Dam shed: nos. 75008, 75030, 75031, 75050 and 75130.

'Austerity' class saddle tank no. 75082 repatriated from Holland comprises parts of Hudswell Clarke 1739/1943 (W.D. no. 75082) and Hunslet 3155/1944 (W.D. 75105) both of which had ended up working for the Netherlands Railways as NS nos. 8812 and 8815 respectively.

Late in 1944 and prior to going to Holland both locos had worked from the Belgian shed at Merelbeke. The hybrid had later spent a number of years on the Tilburg-Turnhout line, a preservation venture which failed in 1981, and was rescued from a Dutch scrapyard for the Northampton Steam Railway.

The repatriated 'Austerities' preserved are thought to be:

75006	Nene Valley Railway	68081
75008	Bodmin & Wenford Rly.	'Swiftshure'
75019	Rutland Railway Museum	
75030	Brechin Railway	'Diana'
75031	Scottish RPS	
75041	South Devon Railway	'Maureen'
75050	Kent & East Sussex Rly	27 'Rolvenden'
75082	Northampton Steam Rly	
75130	North Yorks Moors Rly	'Antwerp'
75178	South Devon Railway	

The enthusiast should note that these locomotives are prone to renumbering, alteration and transfers between railways. There are many other preserved examples which were not supplied to the W.D. and so have not ventured outside Britain.

(Illustration on page 9)

United States Army Transport Corps 'Over Here'

0-6-0T ex-Southern Railway Nos. 64, 65, 70, & 72, ex-JZ (Jugoslavian Railways) No. 62.669

Standard gauge. The four ex-Southern Railway locos are works nos. 4432, 4441, 4433 and 4446 respectively, all built in 1943 by the Vulcan Iron Works, Philadelphia for the U.S. Army Transport Corps to use in Europe. They were later purchased by the Southern Railway for service on Southampton Docks.

No. 64 is on the Bluebell Railway restored as 30064 in green livery, whilst the Keighley & Worth Valley Railway run no. 72 in an American livery of black and tan with a silver smokebox.

Nos. 65 and 70 were taken into S.R Departmental stock as DS237 'Maunsell' and DS238 'Wainwright' and worked at Ashford before being purchased for preservation by the Kent & East Sussex Railway, where a black livery in usually carried.

The former Jugoslavian loco, JZ no. 62.699, built by Duro Dakovic at Slavonski Brod, was purchased by a group of Swanage Railway members in 1990. It was originally believed to require very little work to return to steam but in fact has needed a full re-tube of the boiler, new ashpan, boiler cladding, valve rings, and refurbishment of many other essential components. It was also decided to rebuild the tanks and cab to UK profile when replacing the sheeting and the loco has finally been restored as BR 30075. This is the next unused number in the BR series - the loco had never run on British metals before preservation.

Former Southampton 'Yankee' dock tank 0-6-0T no. 30064 performs some shunting on the Bluebell Railway.

DS238 'Wainwright' on the Kent and East Sussex Railway.

The Keighley and Worth Valley Railway turned out dock tank no. 72 in an American livery of light brown with a silver smokebox. In this scene it is just outside Keighley station handling the coaching stock movements in company with a former Manchester Ship Canal locomotive.

2-8-0   USATC Class S.160
SEK   (Greek Railways) No. 575,
PKP   (Polish Railways) Class Tr-203
         USATC Nos. 5820, 2089 & 2253,
MÁV   (Hungarian Railways)
         Nos. 411.144 and 411.388,
Fushun Coal Mine (China) USATC No. 5197

Standard gauge. The S.160 class was designed to fit within the British loading gauge so that the locos could be used in the U.K. before going abroad and would then also be useable anywhere else in Europe. Some remained in Britain, but with a reputation for collapsing fireboxes they were decidedly unpopular and none lasted long enough to be preserved. Numerous others in parts of Europe and China remained in service until relatively recently though and have been obtained for service in the UK.

The first of the S.160 class to be seen in Britain for many years was ex-USATC no. 5820 (Lima 8758/1945), which had been sent to Poland and was taken into PKP class Tr-203 as no. Tr-203.474. After withdrawal the Keighley and Worth Valley Railway obtained the loco and restored it to USATC grey livery, and at least one of its former drivers from Poland has had a hand at the regulator again. This loco has also featured many times on film, it's appearance in 'Yanks' being one of the most celebrated.

Baldwin 70533, built in 1944, went to Italy with the USATC (no. 3278), becoming Italian State Railways no. 736.073 but was bought by Greece's Hellenic State Railways in 1960, along with twenty-four others absorbed into class Theta delta. The total of 52 locos (Greece already had 27) made this the largest Greek class. After protracted negotiations Td 575 returned to Britain in 1984 with a pair of WD 2-10-0s and is now at Ropley on the Mid-Hants

Former USATC no. 3278 in a new guise as no. 701 'Franklin D. Roosevelt' takes a passenger train out of Ropley towards Alton on the Mid-Hants Railway.

Railway restored in Longmoor Military Railway WD blue livery as 'Franklin D. Roosevelt'.

The North Yorkshire Moors Railway has also obtained two members of the class, both of which had formerly worked in Britain. 2089 was based at the LMS Toton shed prior to D-Day whilst 2253 saw service on the LNER. In Poland no. 2089 carried PKP identity Tr-203.288 and 2253 was Tr-203.289. By 1993 no. 2253 was back in operation but incorrect tyre profiles meant that the wheels had to be returned soon afterwards.

Two further examples have been obtained from Hungary, former MÁV class 411. The Hungarians did a certain amount of rebuilding, including raising the height of the cab and chimney beyond the British loading gauge and, though still under restoration at the time of writing, it is believed that these will be returned to the UK operating profile. The engines concerned are 411.144 (former USATC no. 6046, Baldwin 72080/1945), and 411.388 (USATC no. 1631, Alco 70284/1942). Both these engines had worked on the SNCF before passing to Hungary.

411.388 was imported for the East Lancashire Railway by Ian Riley in the 1990s, travelling by road in a dismantled form. 411.144 was last noted dismantled at the Birmingham Railway Museum.

Finally, Derek Foster managed to obtain a member of the class, no. 5197, that ended up in China working at Fushun open cast coal mine. It was built by Lima in 1942 but the works plates are missing and nothing is known of the loco's early history. In China the number carried was $KD^6.463$. Departure from Xingiang port was on October 10th 1995 on board a German container ship, the MV Kornat. Restoration was completed at the Llangollen Railway in February 2000, but since then 5197 has been sold and is now based at Cheddleton in Staffordshire.

2-8-0 No. 701, Mid-Hants Railway

The Keighley & Worth Valley Railway's USATC 2-8-0 no. 5820 at the head of a passenger train in Keighley station.

Exports to the Empire, Repatriated

0-4-0VB Tram No. 2 'John Bull'

Standard gauge. Works no. 2464. Built in 1885 by Beyer Peacock to 'Wilkinson's Patent' design and sent to Sydney, Australia for demonstration purposes. 'John Bull' returned after a short antipodean stay to become the shunter at the company's works in Gorton for seventy years. Later this tram loco was retired to the National Tramway Museum at Crich, where it is still steamed from time to time.

Right: Tram loco 'John Bull' in the depot at the National Tramway Museum at Crich in Derbyshire.

4-4-0 No. 3157 P.R. 'SPS' class

5'6" gauge. Works no. 3064. Built in 1911 by Vulcan Foundry, originally for the North Western Railway of India for use on express mail trains. After withdrawal from active service on Pakistan Railway, 3157 was donated by the President of Pakistan and restored at Lahore before running under its own steam to Karachi docks. 3157 was unloaded at Liverpool on 26th April 1982 and transported to the Liverpool Road Station Museum in Manchester, where it is now on display in the Power Hall.

0-4-0ST 'Barrington'

Standard gauge. 'Barrington' was built in 1921 for the Bombay Harbour Improvement Trust by the Avonside Engine Co., works no. 1875. At some later date it was repatriated in a group of eight Avonside locos and went into industrial service at quarry and cement works until preserved by the East Anglian Railway Museum in 1971. After a spell on the Great Central Railway from 1974-88, 'Barrington' was acquired by the Colne Valley Railway and was given a long-term overhaul, returning to traffic on May 14th 2000.
(Not illustrated).

The Power Hall of Manchester's excellent science museum, housed in the historic Liverpool Road Station building, was virtually assembled around Pakistan Railways 4-4-0 no. 3157 in the early 1980s as it stood on it's 5'6" gauge track.

0-4-0T No. 3 'Rishra'

2 foot gauge. Works no. 2007. Built in 1921 by Messrs. Baguley and exported to India for use at the Pulta Pumping Station, Calcutta Water Works. In 1963 no. 3 was restored at Rishra works and returned to Britain, since when most of the time has been spent on the Leighton Buzzard Narrow Gauge Railway.

Right: 'Rishra' at the Stonehenge terminus of the Leighton Buzzard Narrrow Gauge Railway, running round for the return trip to Pages Park.

One of only three steam railcars in Britain, and a rare multiple-unit example at that, is this 3-car Sentinel unit recovered from the Egyptian State Railways for the Buckinghamshire Steam Centre in 1986.

3-car Train Set, Egyptian State Railways No. 5208

Standard gauge. Sentinel 9418/1950. One of the more unusual items to have been repatriated to Britain by the British Overseas Railways Historical Trust is former Egyptian State Railways three-unit railcar set no. 5208, one of ten such steam trains supplied by Sentinel. Following arrival in Britain, the railcar found a home at the Buckinghamshire Railway Centre, where it is to be returned to running order.

4-8-4 No. 607, CNR class KF

Standard gauge. The class KF 4-8-4 appeared towards the end of the era of Britain's influence in China, constructed in 1935 by Vulcan Foundry Ltd. for the Chinese National Railways to a powerful, robust design by Col. K. Cantlie, Technical Advisor to the Chinese Minister of Railways. No. 607 was the Vulcan Foundry's works number 4674.

The twenty-four locos of the class were paid for out of the

Boxer Indemnity Fund, and put to work on the lightly graded Canton-Hankow and Nanking-Shanghai routes where the wheel arrangement and a twelve-wheel tender spread the 192 tons weight in working order.

No. 607 went into store in 1939 but was brought back into use in 1954 and worked another 20 years until 1974, shedded at Shanghai. As a gesture of friendship the People's Republic subsequently donated the loco to the National Railway Museum in 1981, where this impressive 4-8-4 represents the largest non-articulated locomotive type built in Britain.

0-4-0ST 'Singapore'

Standard gauge. Built in 1936 by Hawthorn Leslie, works no. 3865 and exported to Singapore to work at the Royal Navy Dockyard. In 1942 'Singapore' was captured by the Japanese and still proudly bears the bullet holes and shrapnel damage to the boiler and cylinder cladding sustained in the battle. The locomotive even holds former 'prisoner of war' status and has been the focal point of reunions of Far East veterans.

Happier times were ahead after 1945 and 'Singapore' returned home to work at the Royal Navy Chatham Dockyard in 1953. After withdrawal the saddle tank was purchased by the Rutland Railway Museum, based at Cottesmore ironstone mine sidings near Melton Mowbray. It was necessary to overhaul the boiler but 'Singapore' was returned to active service at the museum.

Truly enormous, former Chinese National Railways 4-8-4 no. 607 was built in Britain at the Vulcan Foundry in 1935.

In 1986 Hawthorn Leslie 0-4-0ST 'Singapore' was steamed up and 'bulled up' at Cottesmore Ironstone Mines Sidings to celebrate her 50th birthday.

No photograph of Tasmanian Pacific M2 was available at the time of going to press but sister locomotive M4 is shown here as preserved at Stanley Holiday Park in Tasmania.

Photo: Harry J. Wright.

4-6-2 Tasmanian Railways M2

3'6" gauge. Works no. 7430. Robert Stephenson & Hawthorn built class M Pacific no. 2 in 1951 for the Tasmanian Government Railway as one of a class of 10, all of which are preserved - eight in Tasmania, one in Australia. M2 arrived at Tanfield in the mid 1990s and is currently thought to be dismantled but it is understood that after restoration at Marley Hill M2 may work on part of the former Bowes line to Burnopfield.

0-4-0+0-4-0 Garratt, Tasmanian Railways K1

2 foot gauge. Works no.5292. Built in 1909 by Beyer Peacock, the first Garratt type locomotive, though it was unusual among Garratts in that it was a compound, the high-pressure cylinders driving the rear wheels, and the low-pressure steam being passed to the forward power bogie. The loco was originally supplied to the North East Dundas Tramway in Tasmania, returning in 1947 to the builder's works at Gorton, Manchester for preservation where, upon arrival, the Gorton apprentices gave the locomotive a mechanical overhaul. In later years it was moved to the Ffestiniog Railway, but loading gauge restrictions prevented its use, so it went on long-term loan to the National Railway Museum through the 1980s.

Since the mid 1990s the locomotive has been undergoing a long-term overhaul to return it to operating condition, including construction of a new boiler and firebox, both of which had become badly wasted. The Birmingham Railway Museum undertook much of the restoration, which was greatly helped by the work done by the Gorton apprentices fifty years earlier. K1 is to be one of the fleet of colonial Garratts available for working the Welsh Highland Railway.

The World's first Garratt has been undergoing a protracted overhaul which may see a return to steam during 2002. Before being dismantled for restoration K1 spent some years on display at the National Railway Museum in York.

Photo: D. Trevor Rowe.

Out of Africa - Garratts Large and Small

South African Railways class NGG13 Garratt no. 77 on display inside the workshop at Pant on the Brecon Mountain Railway.

2-6-2+2-6-2T SAR Class NGG13
Nos. 77 and 82

2 foot gauge. This class was built for the South African Railways lines in Natal and the Port Elizabeth - Avontuur route and has a most unusual feature in that the driver can sit outside the loco! There is a swivelling seat which swings out of the cab to allow more room for the fireman. Although these count as the small Garratts referred to in the heading to this section they are substantial locomotives with a boiler as large as many standard gauge locos and a power output to match. The weight in working order is over 60 tons but the Garratt wheel arrangement gives an axle load of barely over 7 tons and their capabilities include hauling 600 tons on the level and 180 tons up a 1 in 33 gradient.

No. 77 was built in 1928 by Hanomag (works no. 10629) and worked on the Umlaas Road and Estcourt - Weenen systems before being purchased by Tony Hills for the Brecon Mountain Railway. An overhaul for this loco will have to be scheduled before the railway can make use of it.

No. 82, also built by Hanomag (10634/1928), is at present stored in a private collection.

2-6-2+2-6-2 SAR Class NGG16
Nos. 87, 109, 115, 130, 138, 140, & 143

Three 2 foot gauge Garratts built by Beyer Peacock in 1958 were obtained from the Alfred County Railway in South Africa. Nos. 138 and 143 were purchased during 1996 and transported to Wales for the revival of the Welsh Highland Railway, arriving in January 1997. No. 143 is of particular historic significance as it

Class NGG16 Garratt no. 138 runs round its train at Waunfawr on the Welsh Highland Railway in September 2001.

2-6-2+2-6-2 no. 138 at work carrying a black livery on the Alfred County Railway in South Africa before being shipped to Wales. Photo: Alan Heywood.

NGG16 no. 115 awaiting restoration beside the station for the garden line at the Exmoor Steam Railway in August 2001.

was both the last Garratt and the last steam locomotive to be built at Gorton Works.

A third class NGG16, no. 140 was then donated for the WHR by its private owners, Robert Horlacher, Harald Navé and Roger Waller. The first two arrivals had been overhauled by the Alfred County Railway but no. 140 arrived requiring restoration work, undertaken in Wales.

Four other examples of these 2-6-2+2-6-2 Garratts are at the Exmoor Steam Railway, no. 87 (built under licence from Beyer Peacock by Cockerill of Belgium in 1937, works no. 3267), no. 109 (BP 6919/1939), no. 115 (BP 6925/1937), and no. 130 (BP 7431/1951). None of these Garratts arrived in an operational condition but they are on display and no. 109 is expected to be the first candidate for overhaul.

They are huge locomotives for the 2' gauge, weighing 62 tons and with a tractive effort of 21,360 lbs.

4-8-2+2-8-4 Garratt, SAR class GL No. 2352

3'6" gauge. Works no. 6639, built in 1930 by Beyer Peacock for South African Railways who used this class mainly on Glenco-Vryheid coal trains. The 160 ton design features a mechanical stoker, develops 89,140 lbs tractive effort, has a length of 92 feet, and weighs another 51 tons when fuelled and watered.

2352 had been out of use for 12 years when in 1983 transport arrangements were made by the Greater Manchester Museum of Science & Industry and the British Overseas Railway Trust. In January 1984 the GL arrived at the Museum and was restored to lined grey livery and mounted on a curved track to show the articulation.

Double 'Mountain' Garratt no. 2352 displayed in works grey livery in Manchester.

4-8-2+2-8-4 Garratt, SAR Class GMA/M No. 4112 'Springbok'

3'6" gauge. 4112 was built in 1957 by North British for South African Railways under sub contract from Beyer Peacock and posesses a B.P. works no, 7827. The loco weighs 187 tons in working order, with a length of 94 feet, and tractive effort of 68,800 lbs., and was built with the idea of replacing the double-heading of SAR class 19D 4-8-2s.

Peter Pratt of the 4160 Ltd preservation group wrote and asked if the SAR would give him a Garratt, so they did! OCL brought it back gratis, although dock fees and road transport are reputed to have cost nearly twenty thousand pounds. 4112 was in traffic until shortly before returning to Britain, so was in good order. It held a current boiler certificate on arrival at the Plym Valley Railway at Marsh Mills in 1982 but unfortunately a lack of the correct gauge track prevented its use. It has since been moved to the Summerlee Heritage Park at Coatbridge, Scotland but remains on static display.

South African Railways GMA/M Garratt no. 4112 on a short stretch of 3'6" gauge track at the Plym Valley Railway shortly after the loco was repatriated.

Out of Africa - 3'6" 'Cape' Gauge and Narrow Gauge

4-8-0   SAR Class 7 No. 993

3'6" gauge. Works no. 4150. Built in 1896 by Sharp Stewart for the Cape Government Railway as no. 390, and absorbed into South African Railways stock as class 7, no. 993. In 1971 the loco was sold to the Zambezi Sawmills Railway, which was later taken over by Zambia Railways, but did not stay there long as the wildlife and locomotive painter David Shepherd discovered the sawmill's relics. President Kenneth Kaunda presented no. 993 to him and repatriation took place in 1973. Upon arrival in Britain Whipsnade Zoo Park provided as near an African environment as any available here and restoration took place near the rhinoceros enclosure. Along with the locomotive, a Rhodesia Railways 'night and day' coach was obtained and has been used to house a photographic exhibition of the loco's life and times in southern Africa.

After some years the engine joined the painter's other 'giants' at the East Somerset Railway, but in 1999 a British Empire and Commonwealth Museum opened in Bristol and the engine and coach arrived there on 19th November 1998, donated by the artist.

Vintage Rhodesian Railways locomotive no. 993, restored to it's former glory, used to complement the African wildlife at Whipsnade Park. This Scottish-built engine, the only 4-8-0 in Britain, now helps illustrate the history of the British Empire and Commonwealth at a dedicated museum in Bristol.

4-8-4 S.A.R. Class 25NC No. 3405

3'6" gauge. Built by North British in 1953. Repatriated by the North British Locomotive Society, this is one of the first batch of ten class twenty-five non-condensing locomotives for South Africa, all others of the class having been converted from the condensing version. 3405 operated on the Bloemfontein - Bethlehem line until 1988 and was stored in good condition with a sound boiler.

The locomotive was donated to the NBLS by Spoornet, the South African Railways, but it was still necessary to find £32,000 for shipping costs from Durban, a figure greatly reduced when the Science Museum stepped in with £10,000 from the Preservation of Scientific and Industrial Material fund. 3405 was unloaded at Southampton Docks after arriving on the Ellerman Harrison Lines ship 'Ango' and was transported by road to the Buckinghamshire Railway Centre. Although of 'Cape' gauge this loco is truly huge, being heavier and longer than most British standard gauge locomotives.

South African Railways 4-8-4 no. 3405 stands on some 3'6" gauge track beside the former Quainton Road station at the Buckinghamshire Railway Centre in September 2002. In S.A.R. tradition an unofficial name, usually chosen by the driver, adorns the smokebox door.

'Kalahari' class 2-8-2 no. 120 'Beddgelert' at Gelert's Farm Works, Porthmadog prior to dismantling for restoration.

2-8-2 SAR Class NG15
Nos. 120, 121, 132, 133, 134, & 135

2' gauge. Known unofficially as the 'Kalahari' class, these locos are from a series of 2-8-2s that worked on South Africa's narrow gauge lines. In the Cape they are considered virtually the equal of the narrow gauge Garratts in haulage capacity.

No. 120 is Société Anglo Franco-Belge 2667/1949, and was last used on the Port Elizabeth - Avontuur route running for Cape Apples. With a 6.7 ton axle load combined with a tractive effort of 18,820 lbs it was considered suitable for the eventual opening of the Welsh Highland Railway and a group of WHR (Porthmadog) members obtained the loco in 1984 along with no. 134. Restoration of no. 120 started in 1997 at Gelerts Farm, but no. 134's overhaul will follow later and will include a conversion to oil firing and Porta modifications to blast-pipe arrangements. Both locos will receive modifications to the huge tender, lowering the profile to improve visibility when running bunker first.

Another of the type is on the WHR, but located at Dinas for the northern section of the line, no. 133, (Franco-Belge 2683/1952) which awaits restoration to running order.

No. 135 (F-B 2685/1952) is located at the Exmoor Steam Railway, however, restoration of this loco is a long-term project as its condition is poorer than some of the others imported.

Finally, another Henschel example built in 1953 has been acquired from Port Shepstone for the Brecon Mountain Railway.

Leading dimensions:

Length over buffers	54'4"
Weight of loco	36.6t
Weight of tender	31.2t
Driving wheel dia.	2'10"
Total heating surface	1,028 sq. ft.
Boiler pressure	171 lbs. sq. in.
Cylinder diameter	15¾"
Cylinder stroke	17¾"
Tractive effort	18,820 lbs at 85% boiler pressure

2-8-2 no. 133 displayed at Dinas station on the Caernarfon portion of the Welsh Highland Railway in September 2001.

Baldwin 61269/1930, a two foot gauge Pacific, shown here as originally built. Photo courtesy of the Brecon Mountain Railway.

4-6-2 No. 2

2 foot gauge. Works no. 61269. Built in 1930 by Baldwin and rebuilt later with a Hunslet boiler and a massive spark arresting chimney. She was delivered as loco no. 2 of the Eastern Provinces Cement Co. of Port Elizabeth, South Africa, for working limestone traffic off the Avontuur line. Although originally in lined olive green livery, no. 2's working days ended in bright red. After a period of storage at Llanberis the loco was moved to the Brecon Mountain Railway, where restoration has included repairs to the damage which caused withdrawal and reconstruction of the cab and tender.

0-4-2T Nos. 2895, 3023 'Moel Tryfan' and 3050 'Gelert'

2 foot gauge. Works nos. 2895, 3023 & 3050, all built by Bagnall. 2895 was constructed in 1948, and the other two in 1953. These three locos were shipped to South Africa, where they worked on the Rustenberg Platinum Mines system until returned for restoration. An unusual feature of these locomotives is the Bagnall-Price valve gear which does away with the return crank arms on the driving axle. At industrial locations these parts of conventional Walshaert's valve gear were prone to damage caused by lineside obstructions.

2895 (RPM no. 2) is in private storage in Surrey but the pair built later, numbered 3 & 5 at Rustenberg, have joined the Welsh Highland Railway (Porthmadog) loco fleet. 'Gelert' has been restored and in use on passenger services while 'Moel Tryfan', is under repair at a member's premises. RPM no. 1 is preserved in Johannesburg.

'Gelert' at Gelert's Farm, Porthmadog.

2-6-2T No. 14

2'6" gauge. Works no. 3815. Built in 1954 by the Hunslet Engine Co. for the Sierra Leone Government Railways with a short wheelbase for negotiating the tight curves in Freetown docks and a raised cab roof to allow plenty of ventilation in the sweltering tropical heat. In Africa the number 85 was carried, but this was changed along with the ventilation when the Welshpool & Llanfair Light Railway acquired the loco, following complete closure of the railway system in Sierra Leone.

Shaun McMahon, now CME of the 500mm gauge line at Ushuaia, Argentina, and Nigel Day of the Snowdon Mountain Railway worked together to modify the draughting of of this loco by fitting a Lempor exhaust, but working inside the existing smokebox and chimney without making any externally visible modifications. The result was that haulage capacity increased by 16% while fuel consumption dropped by 10% and the cost of modification was recovered in 30 days of operation! Similar modifications have since been made to other locomotives on the W&LLR and elsewhere.

Top: No. 14 at Llanfair Caerinion in September 1999, running round a pair of the relatively modern Sierra Leone coaches.

Right: On 15th April 1971 Sierra Leone Railways no. 85 was seen standing outside the Fisher Lane depot in Freetown.
Photo: D. Trevor Rowe.

0-6-0WT 'Katie'

600 mm gauge. Works no. 3872. 'Katie' was built in 1931 by Arn Jung and sent to work in the Cameroon, on Africa's western coast as Cameroons Development Corporation no. 201. After arrival in Britain in 1973 she was kept at the Great Bush Railway. She was later restored by Alan Keef and on 16th August 1980 arrived at the Bredgar & Wormshill Light Railway, where she is currently used on public open days.

0-6-0T No. 5 'Elf'

600 mm gauge. Works no. 12740. Built in 1936 by Orenstein & Koppel and also exported to the Cameroon to work for the Development Corporation, 'Elf' is one of the few wood-burning locos in Britain.

Since arriving in 1973, a thorough restoration job has been done at the Leighton Buzzard Narrow Gauge Railway and 'Elf' is one of the regular haulers on the railway.

Above: The pretty Arn Jung 0-6-0WT 'Katie' rests in a wooded glade on the Bredgar and Wormshill Railway.

Left: Orenstein & Koppel 0-6-0T 'Elf' receives attention inside the confines of the shed at Pages Park, Leighton Buzzard, shortly after restoration.

In this view 'Elf' is being prepared for handling the day's passenger trains at Page's Park station.

Peckett 0-4-2T 'Karen' carries a light green livery with Selukwe Peak Light Railway lettering on the right hand side tank and 'Rhodesia Chrome Mines Ltd' on the left. Shortly after restoration in the 1980s she is seen passing Gelert's Farm Works on the Welsh Highland Railway at Porthmadog.

0-4-2T No. 7 'Karen'

'Karen' was built new for the 2 foot gauge Selukwe Peak Light Railway serving the Rhodesia Chrome Mines in what is now Zimbabwe and was the third of three similar locomotives supplied by Peckett to Selukwe. She was constructed in 1942, works no. 2024, and delivered that year, evidently shipped out at a time when the Merchant Navy was under threat from enemy action, so perhaps indicating that the output from the mine was important for the war effort.

The SPLR is approximately seven miles long with sharp curves and 1 in 45 gradients up which the Pecketts hauled trains of 70-80 tons. All three 0-4-2Ts worked until around 1967 and were preserved, two of them in museums at Umtali and Kadoma but 'Karen', in the ownership of Andrew Turk, was brought back to Britain. After passing through the hands of Sir Bill McAlpine she was purchased in 1975 by a group of Welsh Highland Railway members. She was considered to be one of the WHR engines in better condition and after a restoration which nevertheless took several years, she returned to steam in 1983. Having formed the mainstay of WHR services through the 1980s 'Karen' was withdrawn around 1990 pending a major overhaul involving some expensive boiler work.

0-4-2T no. 7 'Karen' had already been steamed but is jacked up inside the workshop at Gelert's Farm and waiting for the driving wheels to be refitted during restoration in the early 1980s.

GWR 6000 King George V's commemorative bell is clearly seen as the 4-6-0 coasts through Church Stretton Station with the 'Mayflower' railtour on 26th April 1975.

Former Zillertalbahn 0-8-0T no. 699.01 has worked on the Welshpool & Llanfair Railway as locomotive no. 10 'Sir Drefaldwyn' for longer than it spent in it's entire 'working' career in Austria. In this view, taken in September 1999, no. 10 stands next to one of the carriages from Sierra Leone at Llanfair Caerinion.

The former Sierra Leone Railways Hunslet 2-6-2T no. 85 pulls into Llanfair Caerinion station on the Welshpool & Llanfair Railway where the loco now carries the number 14.

Garratts in North Devon. Four of the South African 2-6-2+2-6-2 NGG16s await restoration at the Exmoor Steam Railway with the boilers stripped to prevent soggy lagging from causing corrosion while the locos are stored outside.

More class NGG16 Garratts can be found in North Wales. No. 138 was at work on the Welsh Highland Railway between Caernarfon and Waunfawr in September 2001, and is seen taking water at Waunfawr, which was then the terminus of the line. In this picture the Garratt is wearing one of it's many shades of green, in this case only on a temporary basis pending a re-paint into a darker shade.

WHR No. 138 passes Dinas shed on the way back to Caernarfon with the Menai Straits and Anglesey in the background.

Above: Former South African 'Kalahari' class 2-8-2 no. 133 in the bay platform at Dinas station.

Right: After years of neglect, almost falling into the sea at Penryn, Cornwall, Freudenstein 0-4-0WT 'Penlee' was restored by the apprentices of the Amey Roadstone Corporation in Oxfordshire and placed on permanent loan to the Leighton Buzzard Narrow Gauge Railway. At the time of writing it is on display outside the Stonehenge workshops of the line.

Brown liveried Orenstein & Koppel 0-6-0T 'Elf', ex-Cameroon Development Corporation, runs round it's train at the Stonehenge works end of the Leighton Buzzard line.

Some of the hardest working steam locos in Britain today are the Swiss built 0-4-2 rack tanks that climb Snowdon Mountain in North Wales, the sound of their exhaust filling the valley as they make the uphill journey. Here no. 2 'Enid' nears the summit in September 2001 with her single coach.

Back in the yard at Llanberis, 'Enid' can be seen in close-up, showing the drive mechanism and the inclined boiler. The Snowdon Mountain Railway is a typical Swiss Alpine rack railway but built in Wales and operating centenarian steam locomotives in regular service.

Locomotives Built Abroad for Service in Britain

0-4-0 No. 4 'The Bug'

15 inch gauge. Works no. 8378. Built in 1926 by Krauss for use on construction trains during the building of the Romney, Hythe & Dymchurch Railway. By 1933 'The Bug' was surplus to requirements and was sold to a Blackpool showman, who in turn sold it to Haymarket Amusements, the operators of Bellevue Miniature Railway near Belfast. Here it ran as 'Joan' until caught in a fire which destroyed the shed. After years spent under a pile of scrap Sir William McAlpine rescued this unique loco in 1972 and returned it to New Romney, where it was restored and is in use on some of the lighter weight trains.

0-4-0 'The Bug' near Botolphs Bridge Road on the RH&DR in 1978. Photo: John Snell.

0-4-0WT 'Penlee'

2 foot gauge. Works no. 73. Built in 1901 by Freudenstein, 'Penlee' spent many years working at the Penlee Quarries until was retired to a plinth beside the seaside at Newlyn, Cornwall. Over time the salt water took its toll on the condition of the loco but the owners, Amey Roadstone Corporation, took the matter in hand and a cosmetic restoration took place at their workshops in Witney, Oxfordshire. Since then the loco has been placed in the care of the Leighton Buzzard Narrow Gauge Railway.

'Penlee', the only Freudenstein loco preserved in Britain, examples of which are fairly rare anywhere.

0-4-2RT Snowdon Mountain Railway Nos. 2 to 8

2'7" gauge. All eight of these rack tanks were built by Schweizerische Lokomotiv & Maschinenfabrik at their Winterthur works in Switzerland, specifically to work on the Snowdon Mountain Railway, which is in effect a Swiss mountain railway in Britain. Works numbers, building dates, railway numbers and names are as follows:

924	1895	No. 2 'Enid'
925	1895	No. 3 'Wyddfa'
988	1896	No. 4 'Snowdon'
989	1896	No. 5 'Moel Siabod'
2838	1922	No. 6 'Padarn'
2869	1923	No. 7 'Ralph Sadler'
2870	1923	No. 8 'Eryri'

The railway is built on the Abt rack system where a pair of racks are laid between the rails and engaged by two pinions with alternate teeth mounted inside the loco frames. It is the pinions which are driven by the pistons, via a rocking lever. On the earlier batch of locos the drive from the pistons is at the top of the lever, the fulcrum at the bottom, and drive to the pinions two-thirds of the way up, which results in a surging movement of the train, so later engines had the fulcrum in the middle with drive at either end, giving a much smoother action.

The coaches are not coupled to the loco, just pushed, so both they and the engines have a centrifugally operated brake which limits speed to 5½ miles per hour, in addition to which the loco is counter-pressure braked by air drawn into the cylinders when running downhill. It is unlikely that events of the opening day of the railway could be repeated, during which No.1 ran away and was destroyed. There has only been one derailment of a public passenger train since on which occasion the safety systems operated as they were supposed to, preventing any serious accident.

There are differences between the two batches of locos, the last three being superheated, and more obviously, having shorter side tanks than the earlier engines. All have a sloping boiler, which is level when the loco is on a gradient, but whose weird appearance when everything else is horizontal has earned this type the nickname 'kneeling cow'.

Diesel railcars arrived at the Snowdon Mountain Railway in the mid-1980s and driver Nigel Day decided to bring the steam fleet up to scratch to meet the challenge. Firstly, no. 7 received a Lempor exhaust made by her driver himself and such was the success that all the locos were subsequently fitted. Nigel Day's regular engine is now no. 4 which received the original Lempor fabrication from no. 7, but modified to a Kylpor (Kylala-Porta). He also designed and built a new oil burner (there had been earlier unsuccessful attempts at converting the fleet to oil firing) and combined with the new draughting arrangements a 25-30% saving in fuel has resulted.

No. 8 'Eryri' at Snowdon's summit (3,560 feet, 1,085 metres), with a view through a heat haze to Llyn-y-Gadain nearly 3,000 feet below.

1895 veteran 'Enid' thrashes her way up to the summit of Snowdon with a full coach after passing the halt at Clogwyn.

No. 5 'Moel Siabod' is seen in the yard being prepared to work an afternoon service from Llanberis. The new chimney indicates that internal modernisation has been made to this rack tank.

0-4-2RT no. 4 'Snowdon' approaching the summit station on 18th May 1980, long before being given a Kylpor chimney.

Main Line Steam From Scandinavia

DENMARK

0-4-0T Class HS No. 385

Standard gauge. Works no. 2110. Built in 1895 by Hartmann for the Danish State Railways, this veteran was acquired in 1965 for the Middleton Railway in Leeds, which completed a total restoration around 1990.

0-6-0T Class F No. 656

Standard gauge. Works no. 360. Built in 1949 by Fricks when the DSB was desperately short of locos for shunting duties. The design dates from 1873 and includes Allen link motion operating slide valves as in the original locomotives. No. 656 came over to Britain in 1975 and is now on the Nene Valley Railway.

4-6-2 Class E No. 996

Standard gauge. Frichs 415/1950. This class was originally Swedish class F, but became surplus to requirements following electrification and the first 11 members of the class were sold to Denmark in 1937. They were an outstanding success and the DSB had another 25 examples built. The reason for 996's presence in Britain is that it is a Vauclain compound, and was obtained with the aid of a Science Museum Grant matched by a huge donation by Railworld supporter Mike Bratley. The Pacific was shipped from Jutland and went to the British Sugar Corporation's sidings for storage until accommodation was available at Railworld in Peterborough for display. *(Not illustrated)*.

Danish 0-4-0WT No. 385 pictured on the Middleton Railway, Leeds, in April 1986. Photo: D. Trevor Rowe.

Danish 0-6-0T no. 656 was acting as station pilot at Wansford in 1980 during one of the railway's celebrated 'Eurosteam' weekends.

SWEDEN

2-6-2T SJ Class S, No. 1178

Standard gauge. Works no. 516. Built in 1914 by Motala with a Schmidt superheater and carrying wheels mounted in laterally sliding axleboxes instead of pony trucks. 1178 was used on suburban and branch line passenger trains until 1959, when mothballed for the military reserve, but was privately purchased in 1975 and brought to the Nene Valley Railway.

The autumn 1980 'Eurosteam' weekend also saw the two Swedish tank locos working bunker to bunker hauling continental rolling stock. No. 1178 is to the fore as they pull out of Wansford station.

4-6-0 SJ Class B Nos. 1313 & 1697

Standard gauge. Works nos. 586, built in 1917 by Motala, and 2082, built in 1944 by Nohab respectively. No. 1313 arrived in 1981 at the Bo'ness and Kinneil Railway having been taken out of Sweden's strategic reserve, and on 29th June 1985 worked the inaugural train to Kinneil. This loco has since moved to the Stephenson Railway Museum, Tyne & Wear.

After working on the Stokholm-Westeras-Bergslagens Railway, 1697 also went into the strategic reserve, and would have been cut up after withdrawal in 1979 had not a team from the NVR visited the scrapyard looking for spares. A few months later at Wansford the loco was back in action. From 1987 to 1996 a major overhaul of no. 101 was undertaken and it returned to service in blue livery.

Left: SJ B class 4-6-0 no. 1313 in the shed at Bo'ness.
Right: No. 1697 receiving maintenance at Wansford.

2-6-4T SJ Class S1, No. 1928

Standard gauge. Works no. 2229. Built in 1953 by Nohab, the last but one steam locomotive built for the Statens Järnväger, 1928 went into store in 1967 following an overhaul and was then unused until withdrawn for scrapping in 1972! Instead of meeting its doom, however, the loco was bought by an enthusiast and loaned to the Peterborough Railway Society for use on the Nene Valley Railway.

Smartly turned out Swedish 2-6-4T No. 1928 running in tandem with the very similar class S 2-6-2T. Note the external water level indicators on the side and rear tanks.

NORWAY

2-6-0 NSB Nos. 376 & 377 'King Haakon VII'

Standard gauge. Works nos. 1163 & 1164. Both locomotives were built in 1919 by Nydquist and Holm A.B. (Nohab) to a design by David Jones of he Highland Railway - in fact the first three of the class were delivered by Dübs of Glasgow. The class 21C, as it became known, was required by the Norges Statsbaner for routes with axle-weight restrictions, which made 376 a suitable choice for the lightly graded Kent & East Sussex Railway.

376 arrived in the UK in 1971, having previously been a snowplough engine used north of the Arctic Circle. After a spell of use in 1976-77 it remained in stored until a £30,000 overhaul saw it returned to steam in October 1994.

No. 377 arrived in Britain during 1970 and was restored at the South Eastern Steam Centre before entering service on the Great Central Railway at Loughborough, then in 1981 the loco went to Alan Bloom's collection at Bressingham, with boiler repairs pending. This locomotive has a claim to fame as it hauled King Haakon 7th of Norway north to safety in 1940 and received the name as a result.

Norwegian 2-6-0 'King Haakon VII' at the Great Central Railway, already prepared for transportation to Bressingham Gardens. The all-enclosed cab for protection against arctic weather is clearly shown from this angle.

NSB 2-6-0 no. 376 in action on the Kent and East Sussex Railway in May 1995, at that time the only tender locomotive on the railway.
Photo: D. Trevor Rowe.

NSB 377 in steam and giving footplate rides on the quarter-mile standard gauge line at Bressingham.

FINLAND

All the Finnish locos in the UK are of 5 foot gauge and had been imported in 1991 for an American theme park in Cornwall, though only one loco has remained there. A proposal arose for some of these imports to be regauged for the Epping-Ongar Railway, however, it now appears more likely that they will remain on static display at Ongar station in Essex. Three locos said to have been imported have not been traced: 0-6-0T no. 792, 4-6-2 no. 1009 and 2-8-0 no. 1151.

The 5 foot gauge Vr1 class 0-6-0T (described on the next page) is represented at Ongar station by no. 794, built in Finland in 1925.

0-6-0T Class Vr1 Nos. 794 and 799

All three of these locos, a standard Finnish shunter, were built by Tampereen Konepaja in 1926-27. In Finland the Vr1 class is restricted to 17 mph when running light engine or 25 mph when towing, due to a severe oscillating movement.

No. 794 (works no. 350/1925) is at the Epping and Ongar Railway as a static exhibit and no. 799, the final member of the class, (355/1925), is stored at Good Hope Farm, Gibbons Brook, Sellindge.

4-6-2 Class Hr1 Nos. 1008 and 1016

The Hr1 was a class of 22 Pacifics built by Lokomo Oy of Tampere over 20 years from 1937 onwards, no. 1008 having been constructed in 1948, works no. 157. The class was capable of 90 mph, though they were restricted to 70 mph in daily service, still no mean feat when they had to make that speed with a train of 1,200 tons. No. 1008 is now at the Epping & Ongar Railway and no. 1016 (Oy Tampella Ab 946/1955) has been plinthed at a builders merchant beside Southbury station at Enfield, Middlesex.

Finnish Pacific no. 1008 on the 5 foot gauge siding at Ongar station in Essex.

4-6-2 no. 1016 is in good external condition, preserved in the Long Somerville builder's yard next to Southbury station.

2-8-0 Class Tk3 Nos. 1103, 1134, 1144, 1157

Finland's most numerous class was the Tk3, a lightweight engine for mixed traffic duties introduced in 1926 and known affectionately by loco crews as 'little jumbos'. Many of the locos ran as wood-burners north of the Arctic Circle, hence the large spark arrestor on the chimney - and the American style cowcatcher is actually for protection against derailment by reindeer!

No less than four of these 2-8-0s were imported, no. 1103 being the only one of all the Finnish locomotives to remain at the 'Spirit of the West' American Theme Park in Cornwall. This loco was built in 1943 by Locomo Oy, works no. 141. No. 1134 is at Ongar and no. 1144 in store at Steam Traction Ltd., both built by Oy Tampella Ab, works nos. 531/1946 and 571/1948 respectively. The fourth, no. 1157 was built in Denmark by Frichs (403/1949) and is with the 5305 Locomotive Association at Ringwood Technical Park, near Louth in Loncolnshire.

2-8-2 Class Tr1 Nos. 1060, 1074, 1077

The Tr1 class was built for heavy freight duties from 1940-57 but also tended to be used for heavy passenger trains. Most were built in Finland, four exceptions having been supplied by Arnold Jung in 1953, including no. 1077 (Jung 11787/1953). The boilers are interchangeable with the Hr1 class Pacifics and like most Finnish locos the Tr1 were wood fired, but due to their size these large engines required two firemen to achieve maximum performance. No. 1060, built by Lokomo Oy (172/1954), is at Ongar station and sister engine 1077 is currently near Sudbury, Suffolk at Steam Traction Ltd.

'Little jumbo' 2-8-0 no. 1103 of the Finnish Railways on the site of the theme park at Retallick in Cornwall in September 1997.
Photo: D. Trevor Rowe.

More of a 'white elephant' than a 'little jumbo', 5 foot gauge V.R. 2-8-0 no. 1134 on the 4'8½" gauge Epping - Ongar Railway in late 2001. I hope I'm proved wrong but the future for this loco seems to be purely one of static display.

Finnish Railways 2-8-2 No. 1060 stands at the end of the 5 foot gauge siding at Ongar station facing the main road. At the time of the author's two visits in the autumn of 2001 this locomotive was in the latter stages of external restoration and receiving a new coat of paint. Even if they don't end up running in the forseeable future, at least the engines at Ongar have the prospect of being made presentable and preserved in a reasonable condition.

Standing behind no. 1060 is a Finnish passenger carriage but on the adjoining track a rake of underground coaches is completely dwarfed by the enormous locomotive.

Main Line Steam From France and Germany

4-6-0 Nord Railway No. 3.268

Standard gauge. Works No. 10745. 3.268 is a du Bousquet - de Glehn 4-cylinder compound built in 1911 by Henschel for the Nord Railway. The high pressure cylinders are on the outside driving the centre pair of coupled wheels, and the low pressure cylinders are inside the frames beneath the smokebox driving the leading pair of coupled wheels.

Originally 3.268, it was absorbed by the SNCF as class 230D No.116 in 1938. After withdrawal this splendid locomotive went to the South Eastern Steam Centre, and later moved to the Nene Valley Railway. In 1980 it was purchased for the National Collection, but will remain at Wansford to work on the Berne gauge NVR for the foreseeable future.

De-Glehn compound 4-6-0 no. 3.628 evokes the atmosphere of the Nord Railway working a continental train on the Nene Valley Railway on 21st September 1986. Photo: D. Trevor Rowe.

2-6-2T D.B. No. 64.305

Standard gauge. Works no.11535. Built in 1935 by Krupp of Essen for Deutsche Reichsbahn, it is a tank version of the German class 24 2-6-0. Active service finished in 1972 and 64.305 went to the Severn Valley Railway, but even the GWR loading gauge was too small for this loco, so a home was then found on the NVR at Wansford in 1977.

2-6-2T no. 64.305 similarly represents a German branch line service running between Wansford and Orton Mere in September 1984.
Photo: D. Trevor Rowe.

2-10-0 DR Class 52 'Kriegslok'
PKP No. Ty2 7173 and NSB No. 5865 'Peer Gynt'

Standard gauge. The Deutsche Reichsbahn class 52 'Kriegslok' austerity locos were developed from the lightweight class 50, using all-welded construction for rapid assembly with the minimum of labour and materials. Many detail variations were produced and the class spread throughout Europe as far afield as Asian Turkey and onto the 5 foot gauge in the USSR.

Ty2 7173 was built at Floridsdorf in Vienna in 1943, works no. 16626 and ended up working in Poland on an industrial line until 1989, when withdrawn at Katowice. During its history this loco was first assigned to Dresden but between 1950 to 1963 worked in the USSR. From 1959-57 it ran on the Russian South Western Railway, 1957-62 on the Odessa Railway and from 1962 until transfer to Poland in 1963 on the Byelorussian Railway. Once in Poland only a short time was spent on the PKP before allocation to the Sand Railway at Szczakowa.

After purchase in 1990 by airline pilot Martin Haines, 7173 was put through the works at Olesnica for a full overhaul and then transported to the Nene Valley Railway, arriving on December 20th 1998. Although the NVR has been been rebuilt to the continental Berne Gauge, during trials the chimney found to be foul of Lynch Farm Bridge near Orton Mere and work had to be done on the track to ensure adequate clearance.

'Peer Gynt' was built in 1944 by Schichau as No. 52.5865 and sent to Norway where it subsequently ran as NSB class 63a. In 1975, after a period in strategic reserve, this loco was chosen for the Bressingham Steam Museum along with a typical semi-circular tender. The name 'Peer Gynt' was bestowed upon restoration.

Kriegslok 2-10-0 'Peer Gynt' arrived at Bressingham in a fairly tatty external condition but was immaculate when seen after restoration a few years later. Furthermore, the ex-Deutsche Reichsbahn loco was in steam and giving footplate trips.

Another 'Kriegslok' has been in service on the Nene Valley Railway. Ty2 7173 was built in Austria and worked in Germany, Russia and Poland before being preserved in Britain.

Polish Industrials in Britain

The availability of standard gauge Polish industrial tank locomotives at viable prices has been a huge boon for a number of developing museum railways needing motive power for modest jouney lengths and train loads. The numerous industrial 0-4-0 saddle tanks are not quite big enough for their requirements while larger industrial 0-6-0 tank engines and locomotives such as Great Western pannier tanks and LMS 'Jinties' are not always available. In these circumstances the 'Ferrum' 0-6-0T in particular has proved ideal. It fits the UK's loading gauge, has a neat appearance that does not look out of place, and spares are readily available. Most Polish industrials in Britain have been restored here, but Polish works have been undertaking overhauls to make locos available 'off the shelf' ex-works, and advantage of this has been taken by museum railways on mainland Europe as well as in Britain.

0-6-0T Tkh 'Ferrum' Class Nos. 2871, 2944, 3135, 3138, 4015, 5374, 5380, 5697 and 7646

Firstly, let's dispel the myth that the 'Ferrum' design is a version of the US Army's 'Yankee' 0-6-0T! The outward appearance isindeed similar but the design is pure Polish, derived from a series of class T1A 0-6-0T built by Chrzanow in 1927. The design was updated in 1929 and again in 1947, these different versions of the Ferrum being known as the Ferrum 29 and Ferrum 47. Production of the latter continued until 1960, to a total of 480 locos and all those preserved in the UK are of this later model.

Above: Tkh 0-6-0T no. 3135 'Spartan' passes the signalbox on the Spa Valley Railway as it runs round its train during a Polish weekend which was held to celebrate the Pyskowice Depot Museum.

Another 'Ferrum' 0-6-0T, no. 5374 'Vanguard', is seen during the latter stage of restoration on the Northampton & Lamport Railway.

Tkh no. 3138 'Hutnik' has been returned to steam as no. A 11 and is seen operating at Scunthorpe Steel Works in company with a Sentinel steam lorry.
Photo: D. Trevor Rowe.

Bearing the Polish eagle on the smokebox door 'Ferrum' 0-6-0T no. 4015 works a passenger train on the Cholsey & Wallingford Railway.
Photo: D. Trevor Rowe.

Ferrums were not all built to specific orders, but the factory built a stock of locomotives without boilers and only added the boiler when an order was received. This means that locomotives and boilers can have separate works numbers but it meant that new locos in stock did not stand around with the boiler deteriorating until an order was placed.

The Ferrums preserved in the UK generally carry their loco works no. as their running number, as indeed they did in Poland.

No. 2871, built in 1951 is at the Bridgend Valleys Railway, Pontycymer in Wales and nos. 2944 and 3135 'Spartan' dating from 1952 & 1953 are at the Spa Valley Railway in Kent.

3138 'Hutnik' is preserved by the Appleby-Frodingham Railway Society at Scunthorpe Steelworks. This is quite appropriate as 'Hutnik' means steelworker, but should not be confused with the narrow gauge Hutnik 0-4-0T class. In addition to the name, the number 'A 11' is carried on the cabside.

Nos. 5374 and 7646 are on the Northampton & Lamport Railway, named 'Vanguard' and 'Northampton'. 5374 had previously worked at Ostrowiec steelworks and is pictured there in steam in February 1992 in 'Locomotives International' issue 17.

4015 was one of the engines built for stock, constructed in 1954, works no. 4015, but the boiler was not added until 1959. Enthusiast Rob May purchased 4015 from the Ostrowiec steelworks in south-east Poland in the early 1990s and it worked on the Cholsey and Wallingford Railway in Oxfordshire before moving to its present home on the Avon Valley Railway near Bristol.

5380 and 5397, built by Chzanow in 1959 and 1960, were obtained from a steelworks at Ozimek in 2000 by airline pilot Martin Bell and transported to Llangollen for overhaul. They had been out of use since 1998, but had received replacement fireboxes as recently as 1994.

Ferrum 47 class 0-6-0T, Chrzanów, Poland

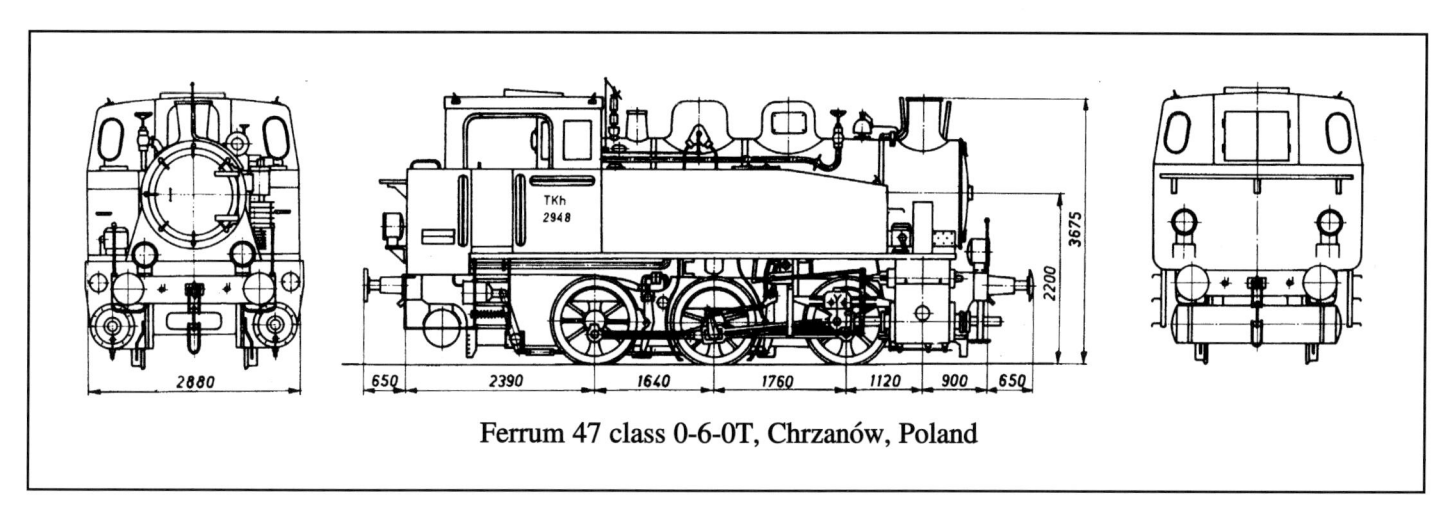

Comparison of Leading Dimensions

	USATC 0-6-0T	Ferrum 47 0-6-0T	GWR 57xx 0-6-0PT
Driving wheel diameter:	1372 mm	1100 mm	1409 mm
Cylinder diameter/stroke:	419 x 610 mm	550 x 550 mm	445 x 610 mm
Boiler pressure:	14.8 kg/cm²	14 kg/cm²	14.06 kg/cm²
Grate Area:	1.81 m²	2.19 m²	1.42 m²
Heating Surface:	72.5 m²	112.4 m²	109.33 m²
Superheater Surface Area:	-	40.0 m²	-
Weight in Working Order:	47.4 t	66.0 t	53.6 t

0-8-0T Tkp 'Slask' Class No. 5483

The heavier 0-8-0T was developed by Henschel during World War 2, at which time the Chrzanow factory was controlled by the German company. The locomotives were needed for a heavily industrialised area of Silesia and the designation was initially 'OS' for 'Oberschlesien', which is 'Slask' in Polish. The design was upgraded and a superheated boiler included when production re-started in 1949, allowing a load of up to 3,200 tonnes to be hauled on the level. Production continued until 1963 to the tune of 390 locomotives, the last 90 of which went to China.

5483 was purchased by Martin Bell in 1996 from the Bytom coal mine and overhauled under contract by the Llangollen Railway. It is now in service on the Nene Valley Railway but is currently up for sale and may not remain there.

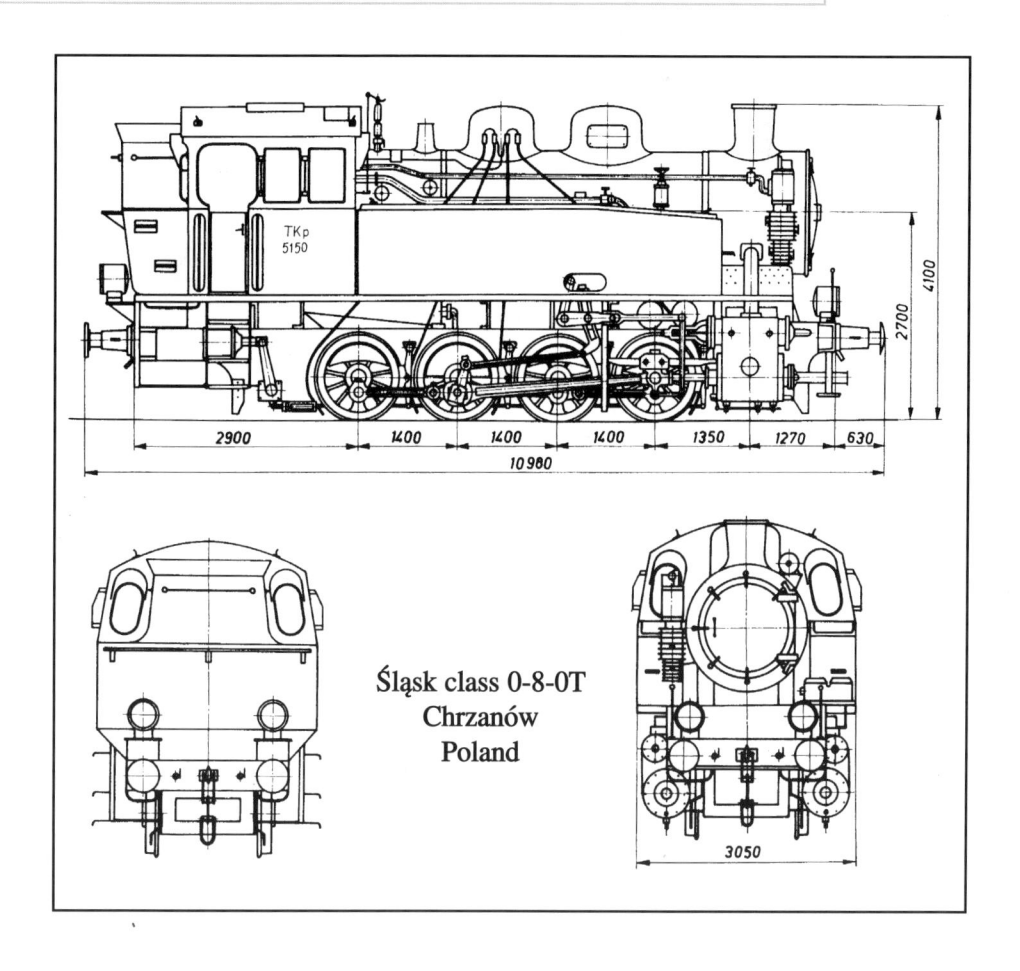

Śląsk class 0-8-0T Chrzanów Poland

East European Narrow Gauge Locomotives

0-6-0T 'Las' Class

600mm gauge. Two of the narrow gauge industrial 'Las' class were imported to Britain in 1992 and initially stored at the Midland Railway Centre. This is a standard Polish narrow gauge class, built in some numbers and exported to various former Communist countries.

Chrzanow 3226 of 1954 has now gone to Boston Lodge on the Ffestiniog Railway, arriving on 15th January 2001 and Chrzanow 3506 of 1957 was moved to the West Lancashire Light Railway in 1998. Both of these locomotives are long term restoration projects.

A third 'Las' (Chrzanow 1983/1949) is privately preserved in Derbyshire.

0-6-0T+T 'Naklo', described in the section on locomotives from the sugar industry is also a 'Las' class.

Above: Two of the Polish 'Las' class 0-4-0T went initially to the the Midland Railway Centre. Nearest the camera is no. 3226, now at the Ffestiniog Railway, and behind is no. 3506 - and yes, the chimney really is supporting the scaffolding!

A more detailed description of the 'Las' class can be found in 'Locomotives International' issue 20.

Right: 3506 again in spring 2001, at the West Lancashire Light Railway, Hesketh Bank.

0-6-2T+T No. 99.3353 'Graf Schwerin-Löwitz'

600 mm gauge. Works no. 1261. Built in 1908 by Arnold Jung for the Mecklenburg-Pommersche Schmalspurbahn, the coal bunker and tender were later additions made in the railway's own workshops. 99.3353 worked in East Germany under the ownership of the Deutsche Reichsbahn until 1969 before being purchased privately and brought to Britain. For some time it was kept at Llanberis, until restored for use on the Brecon Mountain Railway. The little four-wheel tender is normally only used these days during water shortages. There are two other locos of this type that have survived into preservation, one at Friedland in Germany and another which had formerly been displayed at the Mohun Outdoor Steam Museum, California, but which has also now returned to Germany.

Former East German narrow gauge 0-6-2T 'Graf Schwerin-Löwitz' clears the cylinders as it sets off back round to the front of the train at the Brecon Mountain Railway's Pant station.

An earlier view of the 'Graf Schwerin-Löwitz taken at Pontsticill when the loco was running without the auxiliary water tender.
This loco's original home line, the Mecklenburg-Pommersche Schmalspurbahn is featured in Locomotives International issue no. 30.

0-8-0T 764.423

A 760 mm gauge 0-8-0T was imported from Romania and stored at the Teifi Valley Railway until summer 2001 when this engine was transferred to the Apedale Light Railway, Chesterton, Staffs. No. 764.423 was built at the Resita works to the standard Romanian class 764 design for forestry and industrial railways and served at the Turda Cement Factory.

No photograph is available at present of this particular loco, but the diagram opposite shows the type.

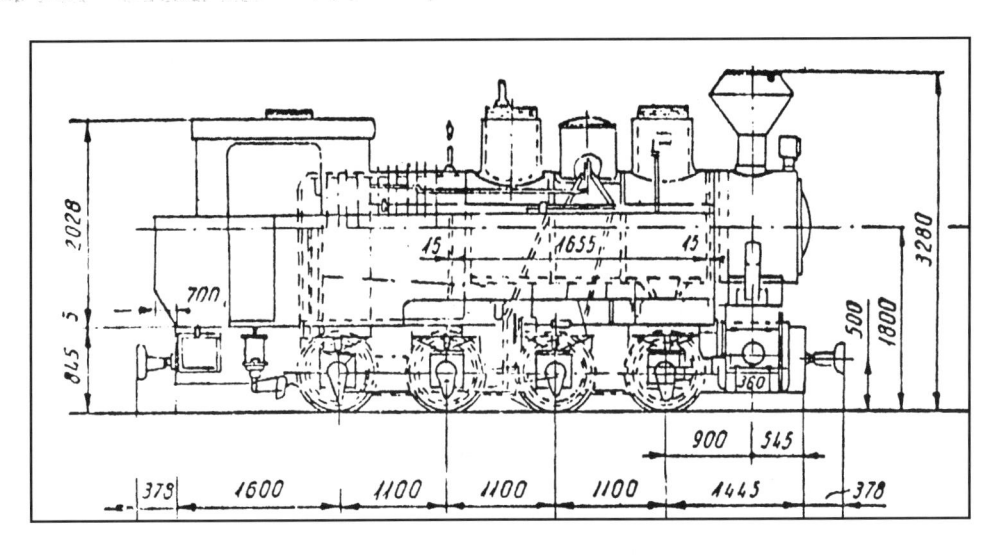

West European Narrow Gauge Locomotives

2-6-2T Jokiosten Railway No. 31

760 mm gauge. Works no. 2369. Built in 1948 by Ateliers Tubize in Belgium this loco spent its working life on the Jokiosten Railway, later being privately preserved in Britain. The owner's wish of having the engine back in traffic is now been fulfilled as no. 31 has been restored on the Welshpool & Llanfair Light Railway as no. 5 'Orion', returning to steam in 2000.

Right: Prior to returning to service, 2-6-2T 'Orion' stands in the station at Llanfair Caerinion.

0-4-0T 'Barbouilleur'

600mm gauge. Decauville works no. 1126, constructed in 1947. 'Barbouilleur' is a typical Decauville 0-4-0T of a type once found on many narrow gauge railways in France. The loco was restored at the Amberley Chalk Pits Museum but is now preserved at Bredgar in Kent.

Since restoration this little engine has made visits back to France to work on museum lines in the north of the country and can also sometimes be seen at gala events in the southern part of the UK.

Decauville 0-4-0T 'Barbouilleur' joins the steam-up at Pages Park on a visit to the Leighton Buzzard Narrow Gauge Railway.

0-6-0T 'Cambrai'

Metre Gauge. Built in 1888 by the French firm of Corpet, Louvet, works no. 493 for the Chemin de Fer du Cambrésis, a metre gauge system in the Cambrai area of northern France, situated near the Belgian border. Unusually for Britain, the Waltham ironstone quarries also had a metre gauge railway and hence the reason for importing this locomotive.

After preservation 'Cambrai' was displayed outside the Talyllyn Railway's station at Towyn but after some years joined a pair of metre gauge Peckett saddle tanks at Irchester Country Park. There is a short demonstration line here, the only metre gauge line in Britain, and a workshop where the French loco has recently completed a long term restoration. (*Not illustrated*).

0-4-0WT 'Justine'

2 foot gauge. Works no. 939. Built in 1906 by Arn Jung and now part of the Dowty Collection, 'Justine' formerly worked in Belgium hauling trains of sand and gravel at Maaseik on the Dutch border. A group of Dowty R.P.S. members purchased the loco from a Belgian dealer in 1974 and transported it to the society's original base at Ashchurch, but following closure of the site 'Justine' was moved to a new base at Toddington shared with the Gloucester - Warwickshire Railway.

'Justine' shows just a whisp of steam at the whistle in this view taken on the Dowty RPS line prior to the Society's move to Toddington.

0-4-0WT No. 2 'Bronhilde'

600 mm gauge. Works no. 9124. Built in 1927 by Schwartzkopf, 'Bronhilde' worked for Norddeutsche Affinerie at a copper smelting plant in Hamburg until obtained for the Bressingham Steam Museum in 1971. She moved again in 1979 to the Bredgar & Wormshill Light Railway in Kent, where there are occasional public steamings.

0-4-0T 'Bronhilde' from the Bredgar & Wormshill Light Railway was in steam at Pages Park on the same gala day as when 'Barbouilleur' was photographed for the illustration on the previous page.

0-4-0T No. 6 'La Meuse'

2'6" gauge. Built in 1929 by the Belgian firm of La Meuse, works no. 3355. The back ground to this locomotive's working carreer has remained a mystery. 'La Meuse' arrived in the UK from the Maldegem Steam Centre in Belgium in 1990 and was restored at the 2' gauge Bredgar & Wormshill Railway and tested on the 2'6" gauge Welshpool line. *(Not illustrated).*

*Jung 0-4-0T 'Ginette Marie' being loaded at Hamburg in 1971, en route to Britain.
Photo courtesy of Strumpshaw Hall.*

0-4-0WT No. 6 'Ginette Marie'

600 mm gauge. Works no. 7509. Built in 1937 by Arn Jung and now kept at Strumpshaw Hall near Brundall, Norfolk for use on a 2 foot gauge line in the grounds. Previous history of the loco includes working for Eisefelde Steinwerke in Germany before being shipped to Britain in 1971, followed by a spell on the Llanberis Lake Railway with the name 'Cyclops'.

0-4-0T No. 5 'Helen Kathryn'

600 mm gauge. Built in 1948 by Henschel to the company's 'Riesa' class design, works no. 28035. 'Helen Kathryn' was used on various construction contracts, including clearing rubble from war-damaged German cities and was purchased for preservation and imported in 1971. She went initially to the Bala Lake Railway then spent a number of years from 1975 onwards at the Llanberis Lake Railway carrying the no. 5. Another change took place in 1991 with a move to Alston, followed by an overhaul. 'Helen Kathryn' is now operational on the South Tynedale Railway as STR no. 14.

Henschel 0-4-0T 'Helen Kathryn' is about to be moved under cover at the end of a day on show at Llanberis.

Orenstein & Koppel Narrow Gauge Locomotives

0-4-0WT No. 1 'Eigiau'

600 mm gauge. O&K works no. 5668, built in 1912 and supplied to the Aluminium Corporation of Dolgarrog for work on the Llyn Eigiau reservoir project. In 1928 'Eigiau' was sold on to Penrhyn Quarries, and in 1963 was preserved and restored for the Nursery Railway at Bressingham Gardens. This loco can now be found on the Bredgar & Wormshill Light Railway having spent all its working life in Britain.

0-4-0WT 'Eigiau' on the Nursery Railway

0-6-0WT 'Nantmor', 'Pedemoura' and 'Sao Domingos'

2 foot gauge. Works nos. are 9239 for 'Nantmor', built in 1921, 10808 for 'Pedemoura' built in 1924, and 11784 for 'Sao Domingos' built in 1925. Orenstein & Koppel constructed all three locos, which worked in Portugal for the Empresa Carbonifera do Douro at Pederido, belonging to the Minas de Pejao company.

The three locos arrived in Britain in 1972. 'Pedemoura' and 'Sao Domingos' went to the Knebworth and Wintergreen Railway, but were split up when 'Pedemoura' moved to the Welsh Highland Railway and 'Sao Domingos' moved to Haltwhistle. Meanwhile 'Nantmor', originally known as 'Fojo', went in the first place to a light railway group in Dorset before joining 'Pedemoura' on the WHR. 'Pedemoura' then moved to Mold for restoration work, including the provision of a new boiler. 'Nantmor' is now at a private location in Herefordshire.

'Sao Domingos' was purchased by the South Tynedale Preservation Society at an early stage in their project to reopen the line from Alston and was the first steam locomotive on the line. Restoration has been a long term affair, involving the manufacture of a new all-welded boiler and extensive reconstruction of the rest of the loco. Early in 2001 'Sao Domingos' was purchased for the Bredgar and Wormshill Light Railway and awaits completion of the restoration.

O&K 0-6-0T 'Nantmor' inside the Gelert Works shed after restoration on the Welsh Highland Railway.

Orenstein & Koppel 0-6-0WT 'Sao Domingos', seen when owned by the Durham Narrow Gauge Group, undergoing restoration at Alston Station, South Tynedale Railway. This locomotive is now at Bredgar in Kent. Photo courtesy of Arthur Chambers.

0-4-0T O&K 5102/1912

A 900mm gauge Orenstein & Koppel 0-4-0T from a private location has been at Alan Keef's workshops during 2001/2002. No historical details of this loco are known at present.

0-4-0T No. 1 'Elouise'

600mm gauge. 'Elouise' was not built in Berlin but at the Orenstein & Koppel factory in Madrid in 1922, works no. 9998, and is now owned by Carl Da Costa and normally kept at the Old Kiln Railway in Surrey, however, in our picture she is seen on a visit to the Welsh Highland Railway at Porthmadog.

0-4-0WT No. 9

600 mm gauge. Works no. 12722. Built in 1936 by Orenstein & Koppel, no. 9 worked at a stone quarry for Carl Brandt of Bremen before coming to Britain in 1970. After a period of storage at Dinorwic Quarries, Llanberis, the loco was restored in North Wales and later moved to the Brecon Mountain Railway where it was intended to renew the firebox. Other projects took priority, however, and with larger locos being more suited to the BMR, in due course no. 9 passed to the Bredgar & Wormshill Light Railway.

O&K 0-4-0T no. 9 stands outside the shed at Pant in company with Hunslet 0-4-0ST 'Sybil' in 1981. Photo courtesy of the Brecon Mountain Railway.

0-4-0WT No. 8 'Elsa'

2 foot gauge. Works no. 7122, originally supplied as one of four locos for the Natal Ammonium Anthracite Mine of Enyati, South Africa. There this loco operated the branch from Boomlaer (Hlobane) until conversion of the mine's railway to 3'6" 'Cape' gauge in the 1920s. Afterwards 7122 passed to Lonely Mine, north of Bulawayo, then in the 1930s was sold on to the Rhodesia Native Timber company.

In 1949 7122 joined the loco fleet of the Selukwe Peak Light Railway, along with the RNT's 'Margaret' (whose boiler is now carried by Elsa) to serve the Rhodesia Chrome Mines. During overhaul at Selukwe she gained Peckett injectors and gauges and parts of the motion from other Orenstein & Koppel locos working on the railway.

During the 1970s the Selukwe Lions Club operated a weekend railway service for charity fund raising and O&K 7122 was presented to the Lions in 1972 by the SPLR. It was at this point that the number 8 and name 'Elsa' were bestowed. The popular charity enterprise ceased in 1979 and 'Elsa' lay out of use until purchased by the Rev. Ted Hamer in 1986 who then restored her in his back garden at Kadoma. Both the Reverend and his loco have now been repatriated from Zimbabwe to Britain and are now active in the Canterbury area.

The loco arrived in Britain in 1989, going to the Isle of Thanet Light Railway, now minus the bunker which was fabricated in Africa but had to be removed in 1996 prior to purhase by the Reverend, due to wastage of the metal. These days 'Elsa' carries a GWR green livery - her first operators in Natal were German brothers by the name of Brunel! *(Not illustrated)*.

0-6-0T No. 740

2 foot gauge. Four six-coupled tank engines were supplied to the Matheran Hill Railway in India, the first pair in 1905 and the second two in 1907. No. 740 was one of the second pair, works no. 2343.

To reach the hill resort of Matheran the line climbs at a ruling gradient of 1 in 20 with curves on a minimum radius of 40 ft. To cope with the curves and maintain adhesion the wheelbase of these locos was made flexible by allowing radial movement in the outer driving axles.

Steam worked on the line until the early 1980s and all four steam locomotives were preserved. No. 740 came to Britain fairly soon after withdrawal and was displayed for some time at Amberley Chalk Pits Museum. The loco then went to Railworld, Peterborough where it was mounted on a plinth inclined at an angle to show the dramatic incline it had worked on in India. In the mid 1990s a decision taken to restore 740 to working order resulted in a transfer to the workshops at Pages Park, Leighton Buzzard. There, at the time of writing, it is in the latter stages of re-assembly with the possibility of being operational by the time this book is published, hopefully still sporting the unusual Matheran blue & white livery as illustrated on the rear cover.

0-4-0WT 6335/1913

2 foot gauge. Works no. 6335/1913. This loco, unidentified save for its works number, is at the Leadhills and Wanlockhead Railway Society in south Lanarkshire. *(Not illustrated)*.

Apart from the Orenstein & Koppel locomotives featured on these few pages, several more can be found in other sections of the book, including WW1 'Feldbahn' 0-4-0T no. 2, 'Elf' from the Cameroon in Africa, 'P.C. Allen', 'Utrillas' and 'Montalban' all imported from Spain and two 0-8-0T rescued from the Sena Sugar Estates.

Narrow Gauge Steam From Spanish Lines

0-4-0ST No. 11 'Escucha'

600 mm gauge. Works no. 748. Built in 1884 by Black Hawthorn and exported to Portugal. The first thirty years history of this veteran are uncertain, but around 1914 no. 11 was acquired by the Minas y Ferrocarriles de Utrillas and was named 'Escucha'. By the time the loco returned to Britain during 1985 the cab had been extended and side tanks fitted, however, restoration at the Tanfield Railway included a return to the original condition. (*Not illustrated*).

0-4-0WT No. 21 'Utrillas' & No. 22 'Montalban'

600 mm gauge. Works no. 2378, 'Utrillas' was built in 1908 by Orenstein & Koppel and imported for preservation on the West Lancashire Light Railway at Hesketh Bank in 1985, having worked previously for the Minas y Ferrocarriles de Utrillas near Zaragoza, Spain. 'Utrillas' returned to steam in May 1999.

'Montalban' was built in 1914, also by Orenstein & Koppel, works no. 6641, as the sister loco to 'Utrillas' for the MFU. After arrival in Britain 'Montalban' likewise moved to the West Lancashire Light Railway near Southport and was restored to running condition in 1999.

Right: No. 22 'Montalban' runs round its train at Hesketh Bank on the West Lancashire Light Railway early in 2001.

The former MFU Orenstein & Koppel 0-4-0T 'Montalban' raises steam at Pages Park, Leighton Buzzard in 1999.

0-4-0WT 'P.C. Allen'

600 mm gauge. Works no. 5834. Built in 1912 by Orenstein & Koppel, this loco worked for Solvay y Cia at their works in Torrelavega, Spain until being brought to Britain in 1963 by Sir Peter Allen - the name was given whilst the locomotive was still in industrial service. The Leighton Buzzard Narrow Gauge Railway has had the loco on loan since 1970 and undertook major restoration work during the 1990s.

Shortly after returning to traffic in 2000 an accident occurred at one of the line's level crossings when a car trying to beat the train collided with the locomotive, bending the frames and causing other damage in the impact. Fortunately the locomotive made of more solid material than the car and returned to traffic after repairs.

Following a long term overhaul Orenstein & Koppel 0-4-0WT 'P.C. Allen' stands outside the shed at Pages Park during a steam test of the new pipework fitted towards the end of the 1999 running season.

0-4-2ST 'San Justo' and 'Santa Ana'

550 mm gauge. Works nos. 639 and 640 respectively, built in 1902 by Hudswell Clarke and exported to the San Salvador Spanish Iron Ore works, Santander. Later they were sold and worked on the iron ore system of the Hulleras Vasco Leonesa S.A. until withdrawal in 1970.

In 1973 the two locos were purchased and arrived in the UK for placement in private collections. 'Santa Anna' was displayed for some time in the workshop at the Pant terminus of the Brecon Mountain Railway pending restoration but is now stored elsewhere and these two locos are not on public view at present.

'Santa Ana' was built in 1902 by Hudswell Clarke and spent all her working life in Spain but her appearance could not be taken for anything other than a classic British industrial saddle tank.

0-4-2T No. 101
0-4-0T Nos. 102, 103, & No. 6 'Thomas Edmondson'

600 mm gauge. Works nos. 16073/43/45/47 respectively. All four were built in 1918 to a standard narrow gauge design by Henschel for the Tigris Kriegsbahn in Turkey but were not delivered due to the end of hostilities. In the 1920s they were sold to the Spanish Government as part of a batch of 20 locos.

Some were sold to the Minas y Ferrocarril de Utrillas in 1962 for service on the Sabero mines railway system, but the colliery system closed in 1966 and the locos languished in the shed for many years. Locomotive no. 101 with an added carrying axle was presumably modified at some point after arrival in Spain or even after arrival at Utrillas. The four preserved locos were purchased by enthusiasts in 1984.

'Thomas Edmondson', now based at Alston, was restored and returned to service as South Tynedale Railway no. 6 in July 1987 and was named a few weeks later to commemmorate the inventor of the card railway ticket system. The other three locos are in store on private property and cannot be seen by the public.

Henschel 0-4-0T 'Thomas Edmondson' with a train approaching Alston station on the South Tynedale Railway.

0-6-0T No. 7 'Sotillos'

600 mm gauge. Works No. 6022. Built in 1906 by Borsig and exported to Spain, where the loco was used on the Sabero Mines railway system near Leon. 'Sotillos' was imported for a private collection which is not at present open to the public. (*Not illus.*)

0-6-0T No. 6 'La Herrera'

600 mm gauge. Built at the Sabero Mines for their railway system around 1937 from bits of other, defunct locos. 'La Herrera' is privately stored. (*Not illustrated*).

0-6-0T Nos. 1, 2, & 3

600 mm gauge. Works nos. 1140, 1209, and 1318, all built in Belgium by Couillet, No. 1 'Sabero' in 1895, No. 2 'Sahilices' in 1898, and No. 3 'Olleros' in 1900. These locos have all come from the industrial line of the Hulleras de Sabero y Annexas in Northern Spain and are privately stored. (*Not illustrated*).

The Guinness Brewery Locomotives

0-4-0T Nos. 13 and 23

Some truly bizarre little engines were built by Spence for the Guinness Brewery. Their size was determined by a spiral tunnel with 2½ turns on a 1 in 39 gradient, needed to link two parts of the brewery. The firebox is cylindrical as there is no room for an ashpan, the cylinders are located horizontally on top of the boiler and drive off a crank onto a vertical connecting rod and the frames sandwich the boiler with the water tanks flat on the outside.

They were designed by Samuel Geoghegan to serve on two gauges, running directly on the rails on the 1'10" narrow gauge, but for the broad gauge (5'3") separate chassis were built as cradles (known colloquially as 'bogs') into which the engines could be placed. The narrow gauge wheels sat on discs on a fly shaft in the 'bog' and the drive to the wheels was by reduction gears from the fly shaft. The fit of the loco in the cradle and the mechanical arrangements were so well thought out that it was not even necessary to bolt the loco into the chassis. The only problem was that sanding for adhesion could not be used as it would get into the gears and bearings, so the loco could suffer wheelslip inside the cradle!

No. 13, built in 1895, is in the museum at Towyn station on the Tal-y-llyn Railway and no. 23, dating from 1920, is at the Amberley Chalk Pits Museum near Arundel, Sussex, where there is also one of the broad gauge chassis cradles.

Right: 0-4-0T no. 13 in the Narrow Gauge Museum at Towyn, having been obtained from Arthur Guinness & Co. who had this unusual locomotive design commissioned for their brewery.

The World's most compact steam loco? Spence 0-4-0T no. 23 on display indoors at the Amberley Chalk Pits Museum. The chimney is at the right hand end of the loco.

15" Gauge Locomotives

4-4-0 No. 2 'Cagney'

15 inch gauge. Built in 1902 by the McGarigle Machine Co., 'Cagney' worked at Blakesley Hall and is now preserved on static display at Strumpshaw Hall, Brundall, Norfolk. This miniature 'Wild West' style 'iron horse' was one of many locomotives made to the classic American Cagney design, from which this example takes its name.

Another example built by McGarigle, no. 44, is at the Windmill Animal Farm Miniature Railway, Burscough, Lancs. and a third Cagney dating from 1904 is believed to have been imported from Peru.

4-4-0 no. 2 'Cagney' on display at Strumpshaw Hall. Photo courtesy of Strumpshaw Hall.

4-6-2 Nos. 1662 'Rosenkavalier', 1663 'Männertreu' and 1664 'Black Prince'

15 inch gauge. Works numbers as per running numbers. All three were built in 1937 by Krupp for an exhibition line in Dresden. They escaped war damage in store near Köln, and worked on several lines in their careers before being overhauled for the Köln Garden Show in 1961, at which the 'Black Prince' was known as 'Flessig Lieshen'.

'Rosenkavalier' and 'Männertreu' arrived at Bressingham in 1972 in the ownership of Alan Bloom, but it was some years before the previous owner was prepared to part with the third locomotive of the trio. Eventually 1664 arrived at the Romney Hythe & Dymchurch Railway where it was given a new British name and re-numbered 11 in the RH&DR stock. All three locos have seen heavy use, including more exhibition work for 'Black Prince'.

Pacific no. 1662 'Rosenkavalier' gets under way on the Waveney Valley Railway at Bressingham Gardens.

Romney, Hythe & Dymchurch loco no. 11 'Black Prince' performed stirling work hauling the crowds visiting the Liverpool Garden Festival in 1984 and has travelled widely for similar duties since then.

Steam Tram Locomotives

0-4-0 Vertical Boiler Tram Locomotives

Standard gauge. A number of tram locos built by the Belgian firm of Cockerill were imported in the early 1990s. They were all delivered initially to an engineering company in Whaley Bridge and were sold on to various steam centres around Britain. Some of the tram locos have tended to move from one steam centre to another when shortages of motive power have occurred and the 'ugly duckling' image of these unusual machines has inhibited their popularity. Identities and locations, are:

1625/1890	'Lucie'	Middleton Railway
1626/1890	'Toby'	Nene Valley Railway
2525/1907		Privately owned.
2527/1907		Privately owned.
2945/1920	'Yvonne'	Snibston Discovery Park
3083/1924		Middleton Railway

After an overhaul at Whaley Bridge 'Lucie' ran on the nearby Peak Rail line at Buxton before going to the Middleton Railway.

'Yvonne' went to the Northampton & Lamport Railway after restoration, later moving to the Shackerstone Railway near Market Bosworth in Leicestershire. During 2001 it went on long term loan to a mining museum at Snibston Discovery Park at Coalville, Leicestershire.

The Middleton Railway's Cockerill vertical boiler tram loco 'Lucie' pictured at Buxton after restoration had been completed.

Narrow Gauge Sugar Plantation Steam

0-6-2T No. 12 'Joan'

2'6" gauge. Works no. 4404. Built in 1927 by Kerr Stuart and exported to the Antigua Sugar Factory Ltd. In 1950 some rebuilding took place, including replacement of the boiler and a new cab, and it is in this condition that 'Joan' may now be seen on the Welshpool & Llanfair Light Railway.

Outside framed Kerr Stuart 0-6-2T 'Joan', a far cry from her former Caribbean home departs from Castle Caerinion station heading for Llanfair Caerinion.

2-6-0 No. 11 Santa Theresa

2' gauge. Dating from 1897, this 2-6-0 was constructed at the Baldwin Locomotive Works, builder's no 15511, and exported to Brazil for service on the Mogiana Railway. Later the loco was sold to a sugar factory with a 2'6" gauge railway system and was to converted to the broader gauge. The name 'Santa Theresa' was first carried when working in the sugar industry. After purchase from Brazil by Mike Hart, 'Santa Theresa' was transported to the Ffestiniog Railway at Porthmadog where she was latterly stored.

This loco, renamed 'Brasil', is now on the Brecon Mountain Railway and an extensive rebuild is to take place involving reconstruction of the chassis frames to regauge her back to 2' and renewal of the boiler. (*Not illustrated*).

0-6-0WT No. 3 'Cheetal'

600 mm gauge. Works no. 15991. Built in 1922 by Fowler, 'Cheetal' worked docks traffic for the Karachi Port Trust until purchase by the Upper India Sugar Mills at Khatauli, where it was given the number 3. The Armley Mills Industrial Museum has brought the loco back to Leeds for restoration and eventual use on a two foot gauge line on the site.

Fowler 0-6-0T 'Cheetal' at Armley Mills, Leeds, shortly after arrival in Britain, prior to restoration.

0-6-0T+T 'Naklo'

600 mm gauge Las class, built by the F. Dzierzynskiego factory Chrzanów, works no. 3459/1957 for the Wapeinno Lime Works, Szubin, Poland. In 1966 'Naklo' was acquired by the Znin Sugar Factory, running there as no. 2 until transfer to the Naklo sugar works in 1977. Withdrawal took place in 1987 and this unusual loco was obtained by the South Tynedale RPS in 1988.

Following restoration a ceremony was held on 26th June 1991 when the name 'Naklo' was bestowed by the Polish Consul General. At the time of writing 'Naklo' is being altered with the addition of a tender cab, part of which is removeable during the summer months, and removal of the locomotive side tanks, there being ample water capacity in the tender.

'Las' class 0-6-0T+T 'Naklo' newly restored after being imported from Poland, inside the shed at Alston on the South Tynedale Railway

0-4-0T
'Sezela No.2', 'Sezela No.4' and 'Sezela No.6'

1'11½" gauge. Works nos. 1720, 1738 and 1928 respectively. Numbers 2 and 4 were built in 1915, and number 6 in 1923, all by the Avonside Engine Co. to work for Reynolds Bros. on the extensive Sezela Estates in South Africa hauling sugar freights. Sezela No. 4 spent some years taking trainloads of visitors round the Knebworth & Winter Green Railway and in 1994 went to the Welsh Highland Railway at Pothmadog but is now receiving an overhaul in the workshops of the Leighton Buzzard Narrow Gauge Railway.

Sezela Nos. 2 and 6 are preserved at the Great Bush Railway at Hadlow Down, near Uckfield.

Avonside 0-4-0T 'Sezela No. 4' performs some shunting in the shed area of the Knebworth & Winter Green Railway before a quiet afternoon siesta.

Avonside 0-4-0T 'Sezela No. 6' seen when sidelined at Esperanza after withdrawal and prior to repatriation.
Photo: L.I. archives.

4-4-0T 'Sinembe', 'Tongaat', 'A. Boulle', 'Isibutu', & 'Charles Wytock'

2 foot gauge. Bagnall of Stafford built a number of 4-4-0T for service on sugar estates in South Africa, an unusual feature of which is a marine type boiler with a circular firebox. The valve gear was Bagnall-Price, developed for narrow gauge applications where it was necessary to keep moving parts well clear of trackside obstructions. Several of these 4-4-0Ts from the Tongaat Sugar Estates of Natal are preserved in the UK. Most of their working lives were spent on the Tongaat Sugar Estates, but they were later purchased by Reynolds Bros. for the Sezela Mill lines and some of the locos survived into preservation as static exhibits at Tongaat.

Some confusion of identities has arisen as a result of name plates being swapped between engines while they were in South Africa. Bagnall 2287/1926 was originally named 'Sinembe' but when plinthed in Natal carried the name 'Edward Saunders'. 'Charles Wytock' was the original identity of Bagnall 2819/1945 but the name 'Prospecton' was on the side tanks when the loco was preserved at Tongaat. Bagnall 2820/1945 was originally 'Isibutu' but had also carried the name 'Robert Armstrong' and has also been known as 'Egolomi'. The works details of 'Tongaat' are thought to be 2342/1928.

'Sinembe' and 'Charles Wytock' were purchased by a Welsh Highland Railway member and were shipped to Hull as deck cargo, arriving in Britain in April 1994. Both engines went to Gelert's Farm Works but 'Charles Wytock' is now at the Great Northern Steam Co., Cargo Fleet in company with 'A. Boulle' (works no. 2627/1940).

'Isibutu' returned in 1972 and spent twelve years' static display at Knebworth Park, until inclusion in the Dowty Collection in 1983, since re-located to Toddington. Restoration to working order was under way at Toddington through the 1990s and into 2001, a major undertaking involving replacement of the front half of the boiler. It is hoped that this interesting locomotive will be operational on an extended North Gloucs Narrow Gauge Railway by the time this book appears, and it will be interesting to see which name is carried!

The current whereabouts and status of 'Tongaat' are not known.

Bagnall narrow gauge 4-4-0T 'Sinembe' plinthed in Natal. The spark arrestor, buffer and dome are not original and will be replaced during the course of restoration.
Photo: Mick Greenfield, Sugar Mill Manager, Tongaat.

Orenstein & Koppel 0-6-0WT No. 1 'Eigiau' approaches a crossing on the Nuresery Railway at Bressingham Gardens. Eigiau is now one of the running fleet of the Bredgar & Wormshill Railway.

The short but delightful West Lancashire Light Railway has a pair of O&K 0-4-0 well tanks from the Spanish 'Minas y Ferrocarrilles de Utrillas' 600 mm gauge system. On 15th April 2001 No. 22 'Montalban' is seen in the station at Hesketh Bank with a newly arrived train from the other end of the line.

The Brecon Mountain Railway is home to several locomotives with interesting and international backgrounds. 0-6-2T+T 'Graf Schwerin-Löwitz' is from the former East German Deutsche Reichsbahn and dates from 1908 when built by Arn Jung of Jungenthal.

Two Baldwin Locomotives are owned by the Brecon Mountain Railway. A recent acquisition awaiting overhaul is a 2-6-0 built for the Mogiana Railway, Brazil, which if it is restored to the same standard as this Pacific will be a joy to behold. 4-6-2 No. 2 was imported from Port Elizabeth, South Africa and is pictured at Pant station on 5th May 2002.

The French de Glehn 4-cylinder compound 4-6-0, Nord no. 3.628, is owned by the National Railway Museum and kept in Nord Railway brown livery at the Nene Valley Railway.

Representing the several Polish built industrial 0-6-0 tanks now at work on Britain's preserved railways, no. 3135 'Spartan' handles a passenger train on the Spa Valley Railway, Tunbridge Wells. The haulage capacity of these 'Ferrum 47' types is comparable to a GWR Pannier tank or LMS Jinty, or perhaps one of the heavier British industrial tank engines. The tidy external lines of these locos is reflected by their mechanical straght-forwardness and the fact that they fit the British loading gauge makes them an ideal locomotive for the short to medium length museum line.

Finnish Railways 5 foot (1,524 mm) gauge no. 1016 preserved at the Long Somerville yard in Enfield. The proportions of the locomotive and track in the photo give no clue to its real size - you could start by trying to imagine that chimney on top of an LMS Duchess!!

'Kriegslok' 2-10-0 no. Ty2 7173 in the yard at Wansford, far from its former home in Poland and even further from Odessa or Byelorussia where it had worked for the Soviets in the 1950s and early 1960s.

Approaching Wansford station with a train of continental coaches on the Nene Valley Railway, Ty2 7173 represents one of the most numerous and widespread European locomotive types. The sight also fondly reminds the author of visits to Turkey, Jugoslavia and Austria where other engines of the same type were found at work on the main lines.

Henschel 0-4-0T no. 6 'Thomas Edmondson' runs over the level crossing departing from Alston station on the South Tynedale Railway. When it was built this loco was intended for the Tigris Kreisbahn in Turkey, but in fact ended up working at Utrillas in Spain instead.

'Chaka's Kraal No. 6' also spent some time at the South Tynedale Railway, on loan from the North Gloucs Narrow Gauge Railway at Toddington. This neat Hunslet 0-4-2T was repatriated from a sugar plantation line in South Africa and another virtually identical Hunslet was also imported for use on the South Tynedale Railway, 'U.V.E. No. 1'.

The Bagnall-Price valve gear and motion details of Bagnall 4-4-0T 'Sinembe'. Note the connecting rod is outside the coupling rod and the valve gear components, which are also well clear of the ground and protected by the motion bracket. Photo: Mick Greenfield.

Above: 'Isibutu' was cosmetically restored for display beside the Knebworth & Winter Green Railway after returning from Africa. By the time this book is published she should be up and running on the North Goucestershire Narrow Gauge line at Toddington.

Right: 4-4-0T 'Isibutu' pictured when carrying the name 'Robert Armstrong' on the Sezela Sugar Estate, Natal.
Photo: L.I. archives.

'Tongaat' plinthed in a park in South Africa, in good condition and with the Bagnall-Price valve gear showing up painted white. The loco also shows the same modifications to the chimney and dome as applied to sister locomotive 'Sinembe'. Photo: L.I. archives.

81

Fowler 0-4-2T 'Saccharine' at Mount Edgecombe

0-4-2T 'Saccharine'

2 foot gauge. Works no. 13355. Built by in 1912 Fowler and purchased by the South African Cane Growers Association, who operated 'Visacoharinel' on the sugar plantation at Mount Edgcombe. Cane was also used for the fuel, as testified by the contents of the ashpan on arrival in Scotland! Since 1979 'Saccharine' has been based at the Alford Valley Railway, and is steamed on more local fuels for passenger haulage.

0-4-4-0TG 'Renishaw 4'

2 foot gauge. Works no. 2057. Built in 1931 by Avonside to provide maximum power on the 18 lbs per yard rail used by Crookes Bros. Ltd. of Renishaw, South Africa. This is a unique loco with inclined cylinders driving shafts to worm gears on the outer axles of the two power bogies, which then drive the inner axles via coupling rods. This amazing specimen is privately stored, and will remain so at least until full rejuvenation has been effected.

0-4-4-0T 'Renishaw 5'

2 foot gauge. Works no. 2545. A slightly more conventional articulated loco with outside cylinders built in 1936 by Bagnall of Stafford. (*Not illustrated*).

Avonside Engine Co. works photograph of 0-4-4-0TG 'Renishaw 4'

0-4-2T
'UVE No. 1' and 'Chaka's Kraal No. 6'

2 foot gauge. 'UVE No. 1' was built by in 1937 by Hunslet to an Avonside design (Hunslet had by then taken over the Avonside Engine Co.), works no. 1859, and worked on the Umtwalumi Valley Estate sugar plantation in South Africa along with several similar locos. Steam was out of use by the 1980s and this loco was plinthed at Mount Edgecombe but was purchased for the South Tynedale Railway, arriving in January 1998.

'Chaka's Kraal No. 6' was also built by Hunslet (2075/1940) and exported to South Africa, where it gained its name working for the Gharbar Chakaskraal Sugar Estates. 'Chaka's Kraal' is now part of the North Gloucestershire Narrow Gauge Railway collection at Toddington and during 2001 received an overhaul following a long period - from September 1988 to November 1999 - on loan to the South Tynedale Railway.

Hunslet 0-4-2T 'UVE No. 1' on the disposals line at Sezela after withdrawal.

'Chaka's Kraal No. 6' on the North Gloucestershire Narrow Gauge Railway at Toddington, newly restored prior to going on long-term loan to the South Tynedale Railway.

The Umtwalumi Valley Estates locomotives were latterly maintained by Sezela and after the UVE lines closed UVE No. 1 went to work at Sezela, where it was photographed in 1970 by Charlie Lewis.

Ancient Deceauville 0-4-2T 'Frenchy' at the Quraba Mill near Bundaberg in 1963. Photo: J.W. Knowles.

0-4-2T No. 7 'Victory'

600 mm gauge. Built in 1897 by Decauville, works no. 246, for export to Australia, this loco worked at several sugar mills in Queensland. When new it was delivered to Invicta Mill, Avondale but passed to Millaquin Mill at Burdaburg in 1918. At some point afterwards another move was made, to the nearby Quraba Mill, where the nickname 'Frenchy' was bestowed.

In 1963 'Frenchy' was bought by Tod Watson for preservation and in 1996 joined the Bredgar & Wormshill Railway in Kent. Restoration work was complete by June 2002 save for the fitting of a new boiler.

0-6-0T No. 105 'Siam'

2'6" gauge. Henschel 29582 of 1956. This 0-6-0T was formerly employed at the Chan Buri Sugar Co. in Thailand, where it carried number 105. After retirement the loco was acquired by Garith Engineering of Wingham, Kent and in 1989 passed to the Bredgar & Wormshill Light Railway where restoration has been undertaken and the name 'Siam' bestowed. It was not originally intended to keep this loco at Bredgar and it may eventually be sold along with 'La Meuse'. (*Not illustrated*).

Former Sena Sugar Estates Locomotives

A huge number of 600mm gauge locomotives were imported from Mozambique in several batches during 1999-2000. The importer is a traction engine enthusiast, but to obtain the traction engines he wanted, he had to take a job lot that also included the locomotives. They have been put up for sale and a number have already been dispersed around Britain and Germany, though sadly many are in too poor a condition to work again, some having been derelict since 1966. With identities missing, this is the best attempt at a complete list of what has arrived in Britain:

Luabo Estate
No. 1	0-8-0T	Henschel 14681/16
No. 3	0-8-0T	Henschel 14019/16
No. 5	0-8-0T	Schwartzkopff 6731/17
No. 6	0-8-0T	Henschel 14676
No. 11	0-4-0T	Henschel 11831/26

When locomotives were transferred between the estates they were often re-numbered and some numbers were re-used for replacements when the original locos were withdrawn, so there are several duplicate numbers. The 0-8-0T are all 'Feldbahn' locomotives purchased from the Germany after World War 1.

Marromeu Estate
No. 1	0-8-0T	Henschel 15540/17	DFB 1741
No. 2	0-8-0T	Henschel 13779/15	DFB 498
No. 3	0-8-0T	Henschel 14928/17	DFB 998
No. 4	0-6-2T	Fowler 12817/11	
No. 6	0-8-0T	Henschel 15551/17	DFB 1752
No. 7	0-8-0T	Schwartzkopff 6728 (or 6828/17)	
No. 8	0-6-0T	O&K 11468/27	
No. 8	0-8-0T	O&K 8356/17	DFB 1656
No. 9	0-8-0T	Henschel 13778/15	DFB 497
No. 10	0-6-2T	Fowler 15515/20	
No. 10	0-8-0T	Hartmann 4300/19	
No. 15	0-8-0T	Henschel 14968/17	
No. 16	0-4-2T	Fowler 15513/20	
No. 17	0-4-0WT	Henschel 20777/27	
No. 17	0-6-0WT	Fowler 18800/30	
No. 18	0-8-0T	Hanomag 8282/17	DFB 1443
No. 19	0-8-0T	Henschel 14913/17	DFB 945
No. 20	0-4-2T	Fowler 16453/25	
No. 21	0-4-2T	Fowler 11938/09	
No. 22	0-4-0T	Henschel 23148/36	
No. 23	0-6-2T	Fowler 15515/20	

One other locomotive has come into Britain, 50 cm gauge 0-4-2T, Fowler 13573/1912, built for the first railway in Mozambique. This line ran alongside the Zambezi River at Mopeia and was owned by the company that eventually included the Sena Sugar Estates. The loco is at Bredgar and is to be regauged to 600mm during restoration.

One of the 'Feldbahn' 0-8-0T from Sena Sugar Estates in Mozambique undergoing cosmetic restoration at the West Lancashire Light Railway. This locomotive (Luabo no. 6) arrived in better condition than many of the others, including the Fowler remains of Marromeu no. 16 standing behind the 'Feldbahn'.

Although the design is continental, this 0-6-0T was built in 1930 by Fowler of Leeds, works no. 18800. Originally the loco worked for the Lugella Sisal Estates but was later transferred to the Luabo, Sena and then the Marromeu Sugar Estates. Since repatriation the Bredgar and Wormshill Light Railway has been undertaking an overhaul with the intention of returning this engine to working order. Photo: A.E. Durrant.

Fowler 12817 is an 0-6-2T which may have been one of the original locomotives supplied for the Marromeu Estate when the railway system was constructed, the loco having been made in 1911.
Photo: A.E. Durrant.

No. 20 of the Marromeu system was formerly Luabo Estate's no. 13 but had earlier worked at Mopeia on the first railway built alongside the River Zambezi. Photo: A.E. Durrant.

Orenstein & Koppel 0-6-0T no. 8 of the Marromeu Estate had already been derelict for three years when photographed in 1969. It had been built in 1927 for the Lugela or Luzella Estate and later worked at Sena and Luabo.
Photo: A.E. Durrant.

Former 'Feldbahn' 0-8-0T no. 10 of Marromeu was given enlarged side tanks when working at Sena and also tows a water tender. As no. 10 was not built until 1919 she did not actually see military service with the DFB before going to Africa.
Photo: A.E. Durrant.

4-4-0 Lawley Class

A pair of 2 foot gauge 4-4-0s built for the Beira Railway were recovered from the Busi Sugar Estate in Mozambique at the same time as the Sena Estates locos. One is named "Lisboa" and the other "M'Dundo". Exact identities are unclear but the arrangement of coupling rods outside the connecting rods identify them as being from the 1898 type F4c batch, nos. 38-45 built not at the Falcon Engine Works as earlier examples, but at Dugal Drummond's Glasgow Engine Works.

'Lawley' class 4-4-0s "M'Dundo" (nearest the camera) and "Lisboa" were already out of use at Busi when seen in 1969.
Photo: A.E. Durrant.

SOUTH AFRICAN SUGAR ESTATE LOCOMOTIVES BEFORE REPATRIATION

SEZELA ESTATE: *Built in Bristol. The Avonside Engine Co. 0-4-0T 'Sezela No. 4' is seen on duty with operating accessories, including a big pole for re-railing errant sugar cane wagons, or perhaps even the engine itself! Photo: Charlie Lewis.*

SEZELA ESTATE: *Nearly 30 miles out from the mill a pair of unidentified Avonside 0-4-0 tanks bring 150 tons of cane up a short but steep section of the Wincanton line. In the background more loaded rakes of cut cane can be seen awaiting transport to the mill. Photo: Charlie Lewis.*

ESPERANZA ESTATE: *Three of the Avonside 0-4-0Ts with four-wheel tenders attached stand outside the little shed at Esperanza in September 1969, a few months before the entire system, which ran through some of the loveliest scenery in Natal, was closed. Afterwards they were transferred by Reynolds Bros. to the Sezela system.*
Photo: Charlie Lewis.

SEZELA ESTATE: *The Sezela Mills had the largest privately owned 2 foot gauge system in Natal. Depicted here leaving the summit tunnel on the mill's main line to Ifafa is Bagnall 4-4-0T 'Isibutu', bought second-hand from Tongaat Mill on the North Coast.* *Photo: Charlie Lewis.*

89

Index by Builder

Country of Origin	Country Worked	Builder	Works No.	Date Built	Type	Name/Number	Location	Page
USA	France	Alco	57156	1916	2-6-2T	Mountaineer	Ffestiniog Railway	17
USA	Hungary	Alco	70284	1942	2-8-0	411.388	East Lancs Railway	26
USA	Poland	Alco	70571	1943	2-8-0	2089	North Yorks Moors Rly	26
UK	Iran	Andrew Barclay	1605	1918	0-6-0T	W38 Ajax	Isle of Wight Steam Railway	15
UK	South Africa	Avonside	1720	1915	0-4-0T	Sezela No. 2	Great Bush Railway, Uckfield	75
UK	South Africa	Avonside	1738	1915	0-4-0T	Sezela No. 4	Leighton Buzzard	75
UK	India	Avonside	1875	1921	0-4-0ST	Barrington	Colne Valley	28
UK	South Africa	Avonside	1928	1923	0-4-0T	Sezela No. 6	Great Bush Railway, Uckfield	75
UK	South Africa	Avonside	2057	1931	0-4-4-0TG	Renishaw 4	Private	82
UK	South Africa	Bagnall	2287	1926	4-4-0T	Sinembe	Welsh Highland Rly (Porthmadog)	76
UK	South Africa	Bagnall	2342	1928	4-4-0T	Tongaat	?	76
UK	South Africa	Bagnall	2545	1936	0-4-4-0T	Renishaw 5	Private	82
UK	South Africa	Bagnall	2627	1940	4-4-0T	A. Boulle	Cargo Fleet	76
UK	South Africa	Bagnall	2819	1945	4-4-0T	Charles Wytock	Cargo Fleet	76
UK	South Africa	Bagnall	2820	1945	4-4-0T	Isibutu	Toddington, Gloucs.	76
UK	South Africa	Bagnall	2895	1948	0-4-2T	2895 Moel Tryfan	Welsh Highland Rly (Porthmadog)	37
UK	South Africa	Bagnall	3023	1953	0-4-2T	3023	Private	37
UK	South Africa	Bagnall	3050	1953	0-4-2T	3050 Gelert	Welsh Highland Rly (Porthmadog)	37
UK	India	Baguley	2007	1921	0-4-0T	Rishra	Leighton Buzzard	29
USA	Brazil	Baldwin	15511	1897	2-6-0	11 Santa Theresa	Brecon Mountain Railway	74
USA	India	Baldwin	44656	1916	4-6-0T	2 Tiger	Imperial War Museum, Duxford	18
USA	India	Baldwin	44699	1917	4-6-0T	1 Lion	Leighton Buzzard	18
USA	South Africa	Baldwin	61269	1930	4-6-2	No. 2	Brecon Mountain Railway	37
USA	Poland	Baldwin	69497	1943	2-8-0	2253	North Yorks Moors Rly	26
USA	Hungary	Baldwin	69621	1943	2-8-0	411.09	Ribble Steam Railway	26
USA	Greece	Baldwin	70533	1944	2-8-0	701 Franklin D. Roosevelt	Mid-Hants Railway	26
USA	Hungary	Baldwin	72080	1945	2-8-0	411.144	Birmingham Railway Museum	26
UK	Australia	Beyer Peacock	2464	1885	0-4-0VBT	2 John Bull	National Trwmway Museum, Crich	28
UK	Pakistan	Beyer Peacock	3064	1911	4-4-0	3157	Manchester	28
UK	Australia	Beyer Peacock	5292	1909	0-4-0+0-4-0	K1	Welsh Highland Rly (Caernarfon)	31
UK	South Africa	Beyer Peacock	6639	1930	4-8-2+2-8-4	2352	Manchester	34
Germany	South Africa	Beyer Peacock	6919	1939	2-6-2+2-6-2	109	Exmoor Steam Railway	32
Germany	South Africa	Beyer Peacock	6925	1937	2-6-2+2-6-2	115	Exmoor Steam Railway	32
Germany	South Africa	Beyer Peacock	7431	1951	2-6-2+2-6-2	130	Exmoor Steam Railway	32
UK	South Africa	Beyer Peacock	7863	1958	2-6-2+2-6-2	138	Welsh Highland Rly (Caernarfon)	32
UK	South Africa	Beyer Peacock	7865	1958	2-6-2+2-6-2	140	Welsh Highland Rly (Caernarfon)	32
UK	South Africa	Beyer Peacock	7868	1958	2-6-2+2-6-2	143	Welsh Highland Rly (Caernarfon)	32
UK	Spain	Black Hawthorn	748	1884	0-4-0ST	11 Escucha	Tanfield Railway	68

Country of Origin	Country Worked	Builder	Works No.	Date Built	Type	Name/Number	Location	Page
Germany	Spain	Borsig	6022	1906	0-6-0T	7 Sotillos	Private	70
Poland	Poland	Chrzanow	1983	1949	0-6-0T	1983	Private	60
Poland	Poland	Chrzanow	2871	1951	0-6-0T	2871	Bridgend Valleys Railway	57
Poland	Poland	Chrzanow	2944	1952	0-6-0T	2944	Spa Valley Railway	57
Poland	Poland	Chrzanow	3112	1952	0-6-0T	7646 Northampton	Northampton Steam Railway	57
Poland	Poland	Chrzanow	3135	1953	0-6-0T	3135 Spartan	Spa Valley Railway	57
Poland	Poland	Chrzanow	3138	1954	0-6-0T	A 11 Hutnik	Scunthorpe	57
Poland	Poland	Chrzanow	3226	1954	0-6-0T	3226	Ffestiniog Railway	60
Poland	Poland	Chrzanow	3459	1957	0-6-0T+T	Naklo	South Tynedale Railway, Alston	75
Poland	Poland	Chrzanow	3506	1957	0-6-0T	3506	West Lancs Light Rly	60
Poland	Poland	Chrzanow	4015	1954	0-6-0T	4015	Avon Valley Railway	57
Poland	Poland	Chrzanow	5374	1959	0-6-0T	5374 Vanguard	Northampton & Lamport Rly	57
Poland	Poland	Chrzanow	5380	1960	0-6-0T	5380	Llangollen Railway	57
Poland	Poland	Chrzanow	5483		0-8-0T	Tkp 5483	Nene Valley Railway	59
Poland	Poland	Chrzanow	5697	1959	0-6-0T	5697	Llangollen Railway	57
Belgium	Belgium	Cockerill	1625	1890	0-4-0VBT	Lucie	Middleton Railway	73
Belgium	Belgium	Cockerill	1626	1890	0-4-0VBT	1626	Nene Valley Railway	73
Belgium	Belgium	Cockerill	2525	1907	0-4-0VBT	2525	Private	73
Belgium	Belgium	Cockerill	2527	1907	0-4-0VBT	2527	Private	73
Belgium	Belgium	Cockerill	2945	1920	0-4-0VBT	Yvonne	Snibston Discovery Park, Leics.	73
Belgium	Belgium	Cockerill	3083	1924	0-4-0VBT	3083	Middleton Railway, Leeds	73
Belgium	South Africa	Cockerill	3267	1937	2-6-2+2-6-2	87	Exmoor Steam Railway	32
France	France	Corpet	493	1888	0-6-0T	Cambrai	Irchester Country Park	62
Belgium	Spain	Couillet	1140	1895	0-6-0T	1 Sabero	Private	70
Belgium	Spain	Couillet	1209	1898	0-6-0T	2 Sahilices	Private	70
Belgium	Spain	Couillet	1318	1900	0-6-0T	3 Olleros	Private	70
France	Australia	Deceauville	246	1897	0-4-2T	Victory	Bredgar & Wormshill Railway	85
France	France	Deceauville	1126	1947	0-4-0T	Barbuilleur	Amberley Chalk Pits Museum	62
UK	Mozambique	Drummond		1898	4-4-0	Lisboa	Private	87
UK	Mozambique	Drummond		1898	4-4-0	M'Dundo	Private	87
USA	Jugoslavia	Duro Dakovic		1960	0-6-0T	62.669	Swanage Railway	25
Austria	Poland	Floridsdorf	16626	1943	2-10-0	Ty2-7173	Nene Valley Railway	56
UK	Mozambique	Fowler	11938	1909	0-4-2T	21	?	85
UK	Mozambique	Fowler	12817	1911	0-6-2T	4	?	85
UK	South Africa	Fowler	13355	1912	0-4-2T	Saccharine	Alford	82
UK	Mozambique	Fowler	13573	1912	0-4-2T	V	Bredgar & Wormshill Railway	85
UK	Mozambique	Fowler	15513	1920	0-6-0T	16	West Lancs Light Rly	85
UK	Mozambique	Fowler	15515	1920	0-6-2T	10	Private	85
UK	Mozambique	Fowler	15515	1920	0-6-2T	23	?	85
UK	India	Fowler	15991	1922	0-6-0WT	3 Cheetal	Armley Mills, Leeds	74
UK	Mozambique	Fowler	16453	1925	0-4-2T	20	?	85
UK	Mozambique	Fowler	18800	1930	0-6-0T	17	Bredgar & Wormshill Railway	85

Country of Origin	Country Worked	Builder	Works No.	Date Built	Type	Name/Number	Location	Page
Germany	South Africa	Franco-Belge	2667	1949	2-8-2	120 Beddgelert	Welsh Highland Rly (Porthmadog)	36
Germany	South Africa	Franco-Belge	2668	1951	2-8-2	121	Private	36
Germany	South Africa	Franco-Belge	2683	1952	2-8-2	133	Welsh Highland Rly (Caernarfon)	36
Germany	South Africa	Franco-Belge	2684	1952	2-8-2	134	Welsh Highland Rly (Porthmadog)	36
Germany	South Africa	Franco-Belge	2685	1952	2-8-2	135	Exmoor Steam Railway	36
Belgium	Austria	Franco-Belge	2855	1944	0-8-0T	10 Sir Drefaldwyn	Welshpool & Llanfair Lt. Rly	21
Germany	South Africa	Franco-Belge	2682	1952	2-8-2	132	?	36
Germany	UK	Freudenstein	73	1901	0-4-0WT	Penlee	Leighton Buzzard	45
Denmark	Denmark	Frichs	360	1949	0-6-0T	656	Nene Valley Railway	48
Finland	Finland	Frichs	397	1949	2-8-0	1151	?	53
Finland	Finland	Frichs	403	1949	2-8-0	1157	Louth	53
Sweden	Denmark	Frichs	415	1950	4-6-2	996	Railworld, Peterborough	48
UK	USA	GWR		1927	4-6-0	6000 King George V	Swindon	10
UK	France	GWR		1917	2-6-0	5322	Didcot	15
UK	Australia	GWR		1924	4-6-0	4079 Pendennis Castle	Didcot	13
Germany	Mozambique	Hanomag	8282	1917	0-8-0T	18	?	85
Germany	Germany	Hanomag	8310	1918	0-8-0T	6	Hants NG Society, Dursley	20
Germany	South Africa	Hanomag	10629	1928	2-6-2+2-6-2	77	Brecon Mountain Railway	32
Germany	South Africa	Hanomag	10634	1928	2-6-2+2-6-2	82	Private	32
Germany	Denmark	Hartmann	2110	1895	0-4-0T	385	Middleton Railway, Leeds	48
Germany	Mozambique	Hartmann	4300	1919	0-8-0T	10	Chemnitz, Germany	85
UK	Malaysia	Hawthorn Leslie	3865	1936	0-4-0ST	Singapore	Rutland Rly Museum, Cottesmore	30
Germany	France	Henschel	10745	1911	4-6-0	3.268	Nene Valley Railway	55
Germany	Mozambique	Henschel	11831	1926	0-4-0T	11	?	85
Germany	Mozambique	Henschel	13778	1915	0-8-0T	9	?	85
Germany	Mozambique	Henschel	13779	1915	0-8-0T	2	?	85
Germany	Mozambique	Henschel	14019	1916	0-8-0T	3	?	85
Germany	Mozambique	Henschel	14676	1917	0-8-0T	6	West Lancs Light Rly	85
Germany	Mozambique	Henschel	14681	1916	0-8-0T	1	?	85
Germany	Mozambique	Henschel	14913	1917	0-8-0T	19	Germany	85
Germany	Mozambique	Henschel	14928	1917	0-8-0T	3	?	85
Germany	Mozambique	Henschel	14968	1917	0-8-0T	15	?	85
Germany	Mozambique	Henschel	15540	1917	0-8-0T	1	?	85
Germany	Mozambique	Henschel	15551	1917	0-8-0T	6	Bredgar & Wormshill Railway	85
Germany	Poland	Henschel	15968	1918	0-8-0T	1091	Toddington	20
Germany	Spain	Henschel	16043	1918	0-4-0T	102	Private	70
Germany	Spain	Henschel	16045	1918	0-4-0T	103	Private	70
Germany	Spain	Henschel	16047	1918	0-4-0T	6 Thomas Edmondson	South Tynedale Railway, Alston	70
Germany	Spain	Henschel	16073	1918	0-4-0T	101	Private	70
Germany	Mozambique	Henschel	20777	1927	0-6-0T	17	?	85
Germany	Mozambique	Henschel	23148	1936	0-4-0T	22	Germany	85
Germany	Germany	Henschel	28035	1948	0-4-0T	5 Helen Kathryn	South Tynedale Railway, Alston	64

Country of Origin	Country Worked	Builder	Works No.	Date Built	Type	Name/Number	Location	Page
Germany	Thailand	Henschel	29582	1956	0-6-0T	105 Siam	Bredgar & Wormshill Railway	85
UK	Spain	Hudswell Clarke	639	1902	0-4-2T	San Justo	Private	69
UK	Spain	Hudswell Clarke	640	1902	0-4-2T	Santa Ana	Private	69
UK	South Africa	Hunslet	1839	1937	0-4-2T	UVE No.1	South Tynedale Railway, Alston	83
UK	South Africa	Hunslet	2075	1940	0-4-2T	Chaka's Kraal No. 6	Toddington	83
UK	Sierra Leone	Hunslet	3815	1954	2-6-2T	14	Welshpool & Llanfair Lt. Rly	38
UK	Holland	Hunslet			0-6-0ST	Austerity class		24
Germany	Belgium	Jung	939	1906	0-4-0WT	Justine	Toddington	63
Germany	Germany	Jung	1261	1908	0-6-2WT	Graf Schwerin-L"witz	Brecon Mountain Railway	60
Germany	Cameroon	Jung	3872	1931	0-6-0WT	Katie	Bredgar & Wormshill railway	38
Germany	Germany	Jung	7509	1937	0-4-0WT	6 Ginette Marie	Strumpshaw Hall	64
Finland	Finland	Jung	11787	1953	2-8-2	1077	Steam Traction Ltd.	53
UK	France	Kerr Stuart	2405	1915	0-6-0T	9	West Lancs Light Rly	16
UK	France	Kerr Stuart	2442	1915	0-6-0T	2442	Teifi Valley Railway	16
UK	France	Kerr Stuart	2451	1915	0-6-0T	Axe	Lynton & Barnstaple Railway	16
UK	France	Kerr Stuart	3010	1916	0-6-0T	3010	Private	16
UK	France	Kerr Stuart	3014	1916	0-6-0T	3014	Molesey Traway	16
UK	Antigua	Kerr Stuart	4404	1927	0-6-2T	12 Joan	Welshpool & Llanfair Lt. Rly	74
Germany	UK	Krauss	8378	1926	0-4-0	4 The Bug	Romney, Hythe & Dymchurch Rly	45
Germany	Germany	Krupp	1662	1937	4-6-2	1662 Rosenkavalier	Bressingham Gardens, Diss	72
Germany	Germany	Krupp	1663	1937	4-6-2	1663 Mannertreu	Bressingham Gardens, Diss	72
Germany	Germany	Krupp	1664	1937	4-6-2	11 Black Prince	Romney, Hythe & Dymchurch Rly	72
Germany	Germany	Krupp	11535	1935	2-6-2T	64.305	Nene Valley Railway	55
Belgium	Belgium	La Meuse	3355	1929	0-4-0T	6 La Meuse	Bredgar & Wormshill Railway	63
USA	Poland	Lima	8758	1945	2-8-0	5820	Keighley & Worth Valley Rly	26
USA	China	Lima	8856	1942	2-8-0	5197	Cheddleton	26
UK	USA	LMS, Derby		1930	4-6-0	6100 Royal Scot	Bressingham Gardesns, Diss	10
UK	USA	LMS, Crewe		1938	4-6-2	46229 Duchess of Hamilton	NRM, York	11
UK	USA/Australia	LNER, Doncaster	1564	1923	4-6-2	4472 Flying Scotsman	London	12
Finland	Finland	Locomo Oy	141	1943	2-8-0	1103	'Spirit of the West', Cornwall	53
Finland	Finland	Locomo Oy	157	1948	4-6-2	1008	Ongar	52
Finland	Finland	Locomo Oy	172	1954	2-8-2	1060	Ongar	53
USA	UK	McGarigle		1902	4-4-0	2 Cagney	Strumpshaw Hall	72
USA	UK	McGarigle		1902	4-4-0	44	Windmill Animal Farm	72
USA	Peru	McGarigle		1904	4-4-0		Private	72
Sweden	Sweden	Motala	516	1914	2-6-2T	1178	Flegburgh	49
Sweden	Sweden	Motala	586	1917	4-6-0	1313	Stephenson Museum	49
UK	France	Neilson	4392	1891	0-6-0	673 Maude	Bo'ness & Kinneil Railway	15
Norway	Norway	Nohab	1163	1919	2-6-0	376	East Kent Railway	50
Norway	Norway	Nohab	1164	1919	2-6-0	377 King Haakon VII	Bressingham Gardens, Diss	50
Germany	Sweden	Nohab	2082	1944	4-6-0	1697	Nene Valley Railway	49
Sweden	Sweden	Nohab	2229	1953	2-6-4T	1928	Nene Valley Railway	50

93

Country of Origin	Country Worked	Builder	Works No.	Date Built	Type	Name/Number	Location	Page
UK	Iran	North British	24607	1940	2-8-0	8233	Severn Valley Railway	22
UK	Turkey	North British	24648	1940	2-8-0	45160	Toddington (GWR)	22
UK	Greece	North British	25438	1943	2-10-0	90775	North Yorks Moors Rly	23
UK	Greece	North British	25458	1944	2-10-0	3672 Dame Vera Lynn	North Yorks Moors Rly	23
UK	South Africa	North British	27291	1953	4-8-4	3405	Buckingham Railway Centre	35
UK	South Africa	North British	27770	1957	4-8-2+2-8-4	4112	Coatbridge	34
Germany	India	O&K	2343	1907	0-6-0T	740	Leighton Buzzard	67
Germany	Spain	O&K	2378	1908	0-6-0WT	21 Utrillas	West Lancs Light Rly	68
Germany	?	O&K	5102	1912	0-4-0WT		Alan Keef	66
Germany	UK	O&K	5668	1912	0-6-0WT	1 Eigiau	Bredgar & Wormshill Railway	65
Germany	Spain	O&K	5834	1912	0-4-0WT	P.C. Allen	Leighton Buzzard	69
Germany	UK	O&K	6335	1913	0-4-0WT		Leadhills & Wanlockhead	67
Germany	Spain	O&K	6641	1914	0-4-0WT	22 Montalban	West Lancs Light Rly	68
Germany	Zimbabwe	O&K	7122	1913	0-6-0T	8 Elsa	Isle of Thanet Railway	67
Germany	France	O&K	7529	1914	0-4-0WT	2	Golden Valley Railway, Butterley	20
Germany	Mozambique	O&K	8356	1917	0-8-0T	8	?	85
Germany	Portugal	O&K	9239	1921	0-6-0WT	Nantmor	Private	65
Spain	Spain	O&K	9998	1922	0-6-0WT	1 Elouise	Old Kiln Railway	66
Germany	Portugal	O&K	10808	1924	0-6-0WT	Pedemoura	Welsh Highland Rly (Porthmadog)	65
Germany	Mozambique	O&K	11468	1927	0-6-0T	8	?	85
Germany	Portugal	O&K	11784	1925	0-6-0WT	3 Sao Domingos	Bredgar & Wormshill railway	65
Germany	Germany	O&K	12722	1936	0-4-0WT	9	Bredgar & Wormshill railway	67
Germany	Cameroon	O&K	12740	1936	0-4-0T	11 Elf	Leighton Buzzard	38
Finland	Finland	Oy Tampella	531	1946	2-8-0	1134	Ongar	53
Finland	Finland	Oy Tampella	571	1948	2-8-0	1144	Steam Traction Ltd.	53
Finland	Finland	Oy Tampella	946	1955	4-6-2	1016	Enfield	52
UK	ZImbabwe	Peckett	2024	1942	0-4-2T	7 Karen	Welsh Highland Rly (Porthmadog)	40
Romania	Romania	Resita	1679	1954	0-8-0T		Apedale Light Railway	61
UK	Australia	RSH	7430	1951	4-6-2	M 2	Tanfield Railway	31
Spain	Spain	Sabero		1937	0-6-0T	6 La Herrera	Private	70
Germany	Norway	Schichau	3063	1944	2-10-0	52.5865 Peer Gynt	Bressingham Gardens, Diss	56
Germany	Mozambique	Schwartzkopff	6728	1917	0-8-0T	7	?	85
Germany	Mozambique	Schwartzkopff	6731	1917	0-8-0T	5	?	85
Germany	Germany	Schwartzkopff	9124	1927	0-4-0WT	Bronhilde	Bredgar & Wormshill Railway	63
UK	Egypt	Sentinel	9418	1950	Railcar	5208	Buckingham Railway Centre	29
UK	Zambia	Sharp Stewart	4150	1896	4-8-0	993	Bristol	35
Switzerland	UK	SLM	924	1895	0-4-2RT	2 Enid	Snowdon Mountain Railway	46
Switzerland	UK	SLM	925	1895	0-4-2RT	3 Wyddfa	Snowdon Mountain Railway	46
Switzerland	UK	SLM	988	1896	0-4-2RT	4 Snowdon	Snowdon Mountain Railway	46
Switzerland	UK	SLM	989	1896	0-4-2RT	5 Moel Siabod	Snowdon Mountain Railway	46
Switzerland	UK	SLM	2838	1922	0-4-2RT	6 Padarn	Snowdon Mountain Railway	46
Switzerland	UK	SLM	2869	1923	0-4-2RT	7 Ralph Sadler	Snowdon Mountain Railway	46

Country of Origin	Country Worked	Builder	Works No.	Date Built	Type	Name/Number	Location	Page
Switzerland	UK	SLM	2870	1923	0-4-2RT	8 Eryri	Snowdon Mountain Railway	46
UK	Canada	Southern Railway		1934	4-4-0	30926 Repton	North Yorks Moors Rly	12
UK	Canada	Southern Railway		1905	0-6-2T	30053	Swanage Railway	11
UK	Eire	Spence		1895	0-4-0T	Guinness 13	Towyn	71
UK	Eire	Spence		1920	0-4-0T	Guinness 23	Amberley Chalk Pits Museum	71
Finland	Finland	Tampereen Konepaja	350	1925	0-6-0T	794	Ongar	51
Finland	Finland	Tampereen Konepaja	355	1925	0-6-0T	799	Sellinge, Kent	51
Finland	Finland	Tampereen Konepaja	373	1927	0-6-0T	792	?	51
Belgium	Finland	Tubize	2369	1948	2-6-2T	5 Orion	Welshpool & Llanfair Lt. Rly	62
UK	China	Vulcan Foundry	4674	1935	4-8-4	607	NRM, York	29
UK	Sweden	Vulcan Foundry	5200	1945	2-8-0	1931	Keighley & Worth Valley Rly	24
USA	UK	Vulcan Iron Works, USA	4432	1943	0-6-0T	30064	Bluebell Railway	25
USA	UK	Vulcan Iron Works, USA	4433	1943	0-6-0T	30070	East Kent Railway	25
USA	UK	Vulcan Iron Works, USA	4441	1943	0-6-0T	30065	East Kent Railway	25
USA	UK	Vulcan Iron Works, USA	4446	1943	0-6-0T	30072	Keighley & Worth Valley Rly	25
Finland	Finland	?			4-6-2	1009	?	52
Finland	Finland	?			2-8-2	1074	?	53

Over time I expect more locos will arrive in Britain and some already here will move site, change identity, or even leave again. I also expect there will be something I've missed and that publishing this book will bring out new information, so I doubt this will be the last word on the subject. Nevertheless I hope it enlightens those interested, makes a useful reference and shows something of the extraordinary variety of steam locomotives in Britain.

LOCOMOTIVES INTERNATIONAL
BOOKS AND MAGAZINES

The Barbados Railway	Jim Horsford	ISBN	1-900340-12-7
The Railways of South America	D. Trevor Rowe		1-900340-10-0
The Railways of Romania	Chris Bailey		1-900340-13-5
The Steam Locomotives of Czechoslovakia	Paul Catchpole		1-873150-14-8
East European Narrow Gauge	Keith Chester		1-873150-04-0
Forestry Railways in Hungary	Paul Engelbert		1-900340-09-7
Steam and Rail in Indonesia	Jack Rozendaal		1-900340-11-9
Steam and Rail in Slovakia	Paul Catchpole		1-900340-08-9
Steam and Rail in Germany	Various contributors		1-900340-06-2
Broader Than Broad: Hitler's Great Dream	Robin Barnes		1-900340-07-0
Locomotives International Magazine		ISSN	1353-7091

To see more details visit our web site at www.locomotivesinternational.co.uk or write to us the address below.

LOCOMOTIVES INTERNATIONAL **books and magazines are published by:**
Paul Catchpole Ltd., The Haven, Trevilley Lane, St. Teath, Cornwall, Great Britain, PL30 3JS